From
Frustration
to Fulfillment

Swami
Sukhabodhananda

JAICO PUBLISHING HOUSE

Ahmedabad Bangalore Bhopal Bhubaneswar Chennai
Delhi Hyderabad Kolkata Lucknow Mumbai

Published by Jaico Publishing House
A-2 Jash Chambers, 7-A Sir Phirozshah Mehta Road
Fort, Mumbai - 400 001
jaicopub@jaicobooks.com
www.jaicobooks.com

Published in arrangement with
Prasanna Trust
No. 1, Nirguna Mandir Layout
Near 1st Block Park, ST Bed Area
Koramangala, Bangalore - 560 003, India

FROM FRUSTRATION TO FULFILLMENT
ISBN 978-93-88423-78-6

First Jaico Impression: 2019
Second Jaico Impression: 2019

Stories and anecdotes recounted in this book are compiled from various sources as well as from my conversations with my students.

I am grateful to all of them

for their contributions.

– Poojya Sukhabodhananda

Preface

Change is the only constant that marks our world. It's omnipresent. If you are a keen observer, the street around us changes – new signboards, ads, people, buildings etc. Change engulfs us. Day-in, day-out.

Time is nothing but a measure of change. The clock is ever ticking. Change drives the past away from us and moves us closer to the future. The present is but a fleeting moment. There's no time in it for us to capture its stillness. Only someone who has mastered meditation can perhaps catch the present.

Change is unavoidable but brings anxieties with it. The mind needs time to assimilate change. When there's friction in that process, anxiety results and this soon grows to frustration. Frustration is like a stagnant cesspool – marks the mind's inability to manage change. If the mind does not move from this cesspool, it deteriorates.

The growing demand for medications to BP, diabetes, etc., tells us that frustration has reached epidemic proportions. Frustration is on the road, in the office, schools, colleges and if one recalls the recent attacks on doctors, even hospitals are not free from it. Domestic discord and divorces, tell us that homes are not peace havens.

Change, it seems, aids frustration. If so, is 'no change' the solution? Is stillness and 'no-change' the same? If movement is behind frustration and mental ailments, will non-movement solve it? Can we not find our 'comfort zones' to steer clear of frustration?

A tortoise beautifully fits into this paradigm. It has a beautiful shell to protect it from external dangers. Any threat, it recoils into its shell. A shell is a cosy place, a comfort zone. But, it can't remain there forever. It has to move. Move to find food, water, mate etc. And, for this, the tortoise has to stick its neck out!

Life is similar too. You need to progress beyond your comfort zone. You need to stick your neck out. You have to hit the road. Yes, accidents do happen on roads. People die on roads every day. Should that stop you from driving or moving on them?

Traffic jams can be frustrating – inability to reach anywhere on time, missed appointments, lost opportunities, road rage, skirmishes

– does that mean you avoid roads? No roads, no journey. No going to school, college, office or hospital. No shops, no friends.

No roads can be fun too. Remote islands can be like that – no roads from anywhere to anywhere. Maybe good for a holiday. Not for a living. Once in a while, it would be nice to escape from this noise, pollution, chaos to the peace and solitude on an island. But, you can't be there forever. The island is a shell – you can be there for a while. Life beckons you; your neck has to stick out sometime.

You'll have to contend with the temperamental boss, low paying job, wrong study course or even wrong diagnosis. It can be frustrating. But, reflect on it. Frustration does not reside on crowded roads. Not in your offices, homes, schools and colleges. It's in your mind. Slowly, but surely seeking permanent residence in you. Would you allow that to happen?

Psychology tells us that there are two paths to any stress. Fight or flight. 'Fight' is good if the body is strong enough. Else, it aids a losing cause. 'Flight' implies escape. If you can move faster or outwit the stress, this might be a good solution, at times. In both ways, however, the factor of strength or ability is underlined. Ability without clear thinking is futile. Result – frustration!

Lord Krishna tells Arjuna in the Bhagavad Gita—

क्लैब्यं मा स्म गमः पार्थ नैतत्त्वय्युपपद्यते ।

क्षुद्रं हृदयदौर्बल्यं त्यक्त्वोत्तिष्ठ परन्तप ॥ २- ३ ॥

klaibya☐ mā sma gama☐ pārtha naitattvayyupapadyate ।
k☐udra☐ h☐dayadaurbalya☐ tyaktvotti☐☐haparantapa ॥ 2-3 ॥

(Arjuna, cowardice is not in your nature. O' brave one! You who can spread dread in your rivals, rid your mind of this lowly weakness and rise to fight!)

A weak mind or weakness in mind will not help in a fight. You need to rid yourself of it. You will have to strengthen your mind. You will need to upgrade to transformation. You are what you are. Identify your weakness and turn it into your strength.

How do you go about it? This book shows you the way. It helps you chart a process to strengthen your mind, your thinking and more importantly, your feelings and 'being'.The content is from my various talks. I have penned it down here for easy understanding and application. Spirituality, mythology, scriptures, case studies, stories and anecdotes are its building blocks. It opens vistas for you to experience growth.

Learn to optimise experiences rather than minimising them. This book offers you to be anchored in ontology and effectively use psychology. If you can love, learn and lead, you will reach a peak experience. To dexterously put these into practice, is an art. Art cannot be taught – it should be caught. Intuitively you will learn to blend strength in softness and softness in strength, effectively leading to change. You will not be a victim of change, but the victor in change.

In other words, 'Transform frustration to fulfillment!'. Please reflect on the diagram that follows and make your choice.

Success

Failure

Tension

Tension

सुखदुःखे समे कृत्वा लाभालाभौ जयाजयौ ।

'sukhaduḥkhé samé kṛtvā lābhālābhau jayājayau'

Success

Failure

No Tension

No Tension

Creativity

Transform Frustration
to Fulfillment

From the Author

Life's like an ocean. It opens out to us in all its splendour and is equally available to all of us.

There are many ways to enjoy the grandeur of an ocean. You can choose to observe its glory from a distance. You can go near it to possibly cool your feet. You can go further into it to swim or surf. You can also venture a bit deeper into it to enjoy a view of marine life. To discover pearls, however, you'll need to dive deep into the ocean.

For me, this book is like an ocean. It purely depends on what you'd want to choose to get from it, if you want to transform your life, from frustration to fascination.

Recently, I saw a movie. Infact, I was seeing it for the second time. Originally I'd seen it some twenty-five years back. The viewing, this time around made me appreciate the finer aspects of acting and draw deeper meaning from the story-line.

Similarly, if you read this book superfluously, your understanding will be at one level but going deeper into it, your comprehension would be at the next level. Please read it afresh with an open mind and heart, it will make a big difference for your well-being.

Discover pearls to beautify your life.

All of you are endowed with some talent or the other. Talent is a natural gift from the Creator. Your investment in terms of time and effort towards your talent results in strength. Talent has to become a strength for it to be productive. Remember that strength is an ability to consistently provide a near perfect performance.

Are you giving sufficient time and quality effort to convert talent into a strength? Please reflect. However, this is just the first step.

A person with strength has to connect with certain qualities or values (inspirational insights) that make a project successful. Leadership is all about the ability to think flexibly, connect creatively, produce efficiently and thus leading profitable growth.

The leader in you, imbibing powerful insights that are highlighted as keywords in the book, helps transform frustrations into fascination... a true gift that you can offer yourself.

I invite you to read carefully and assimilate the leadership equations, self-correction tools, the essence of the stories related to being a light unto oneself, the significance of the mystic key, barber nyaya... so that their respective icons listed in the glossary may assist you in reframing your own understanding.

This book consists gems drawn from Indian culture, mythological insights, case histories from actual corporate scenarios, contemporary anecdotes and stories. A reference from traditional Nyaya shastra is presented non-religiously, for application in the corporate set up, family and individual life, for self-upliftment.

This book is a key to tapping unlimited ontological perceptions. I invite you to transcend your limited perceptions.

With Blessings,
Poojya Sukhabodhananda

Contents

From Physiology to
Psychology to Ontology

Ontology is a function of bringing a higher dimension of living called 'metaphysics' to impact, shape and lead an individual, group or an enterprise towards achieving not just growth but profitable growth.

This form of management calls for humility and clarity to understand authority and use authority effectively to create a harmonious working team.

In today's paradigm, however, traditional hierarchical structures are slowly transforming into more democratised systems, with work cultures shifting towards a bottom-up approach that places a great deal of value in inclusive decision making. Team members want their voices heard. Superiors do not wield all the power.

Such bottom-up approach impacts the value systems of businesses and corporate cultures in many ways. It transforms a faceless employee into an individual and an authoritative manager into an experienced collaborator. This means that an individual's personal growth and transformation is as important to the company's productivity and profitability, as their professional capacity to perform tasks and achieve targets.

Management, the art of leading people towards a common goal, therefore, must take on new dimensions. It must play a facilitative role in the transformation of an employee across many layers of growth. And this necessitates a holistic approach to management, rooted in personal discovery and empowerment. Such an approach must address the intellectual and emotional layers of an individual. It must also include a much subtler and often overlooked layer of employee development: spiritual understanding of the human condition.

Why is this important? The development, growth and management of any enterprise is entirely governed by human interactions and relationships. We all must deal with an angry boss or a difficult co-worker and at the same time meet the target. In the process, not miss the human relationships that we have built which requires constant strengthening.

So, what lies at the very foundation in the way we behave, interact, work and develop to achieve our targets? What is the real cause behind the anger of that angry boss? What emotions and complexities are there beneath the smooth facade of those business associates with whom we are trying to close a deal?

Finding the solutions to these questions, as with any question relating to the human condition, requires us to develop a certain quality: the 'Quality of Awareness'.

'To be or not to be' is not the Question

The question is, in fact, how to be aware. Shakespeare's legendary line, 'to be or not to be, that is the question' implies life is an option that we have. Ancient wisdom from the Vedas states that we are eternal. The *atma* (soul), which is pure consciousness, is eternal. Material existence, however, shrouds it with ignorance. And the goal of a spiritual seeker should be to develop the awareness that removes this ignorance so that she realises the joy of her true self. In this material world, life is a gift to be cherished, an opportunity to get closer to divinity, free ourselves of the trappings of ignorance and attain liberation from endless cycles of birth and death.

Therefore, the question is not 'to be or not to be' but rather, how to be aware, so that you can manage yourself and lead happy, peaceful life free from misery and pain.

As you start acquiring spiritual awareness, you will see that to live life is to be related to life. The more you deepen your awareness, the greater is your relationship to life. The more you relate to life intelligently, the more life becomes beautiful and vibrant. In order to be related to life, there are three important dimensions that you must explore.

Firstly, you should know how to relate to the world of objects. Secondly, you must know how to relate to the world of people. And thirdly, you must know how to establish a relationship with your own self. These are the three important dimensions of life.

Reflection Point

Can you practice giving a prayerful pause, prayerful shock and prayerful direction to your lives?

Learn to increase your awareness with reference to:

◆ World of Objects

◆ World of People and

◆ Your Own Self

The World of Objects
– a Vibrant World

If you relate to the world of objects unwisely, you will fall into misery and unhappiness. The Veda says that with reference to the world of objects, one should be mathematical. It does not use the word mathematics, but I am using the word to convey an idea clearly. What I mean is, you must be scientific; you must be objective in relationship to the world of objects. And to be objective, you must be mathematical, in the sense that the world of objects has utility and you should exercise your wisdom to make use of it. With reference to the world of objects, you must relate in a detached way, or else the world starts controlling you, instead of you controlling the world.

कूर्माङ्गन्यायः

The maxim of the tortoise limb movement.

A tortoise projects its limbs, i.e., its legs and neck, for some purpose, and draws them in, when that purpose is met, or any danger is sensed.

Similarly, a sensible person will be like a tortoise and exhibits his power only when there is an opportunity or necessity for it.

Hence self-control of senses is emphasised.

I know a person who was depressed because his profits were soaring. His anxiety bordered on whether his children would sustain the empire he had built. I had to counsel him on his anxieties. This is what happens if you are not objective in relation to the world of objects. You can be extremely successful externally, but be hopelessly miserable inwardly. Happiness does not lie in the world of objects.

If you say, happiness is a quality of an object, anybody indulging in the object must be happy. If heat is the quality of fire, anyone who puts his finger into the fire experiences heat. So also, if people feel happiness as quality of an object, anybody indulging in that object must be happy. But, if a rasgulla (an Indian sweet) is a source of happiness for one person, for the other it may not be so. If smoking is a source of happiness for one, it may be a source of unhappiness for another. There is no object which is a universal source of happiness. Therefore, objectivity is important in the world of objects.

Cultivate this objectivity as much as possible and you will learn to use it in your approach in management. Objectivity and detachment will help you in many of your managerial challenges. When subjective views and personal feelings are set aside, new avenues for problem-solving and conflict resolution open up. There is space for creativity.

> 66
>
> Subjectivity limits us to the boundaries of our own experiences. Objectivity has the potential to reveal possibilities. 99

Thus, the world of objects requires objectivity, the world of psychology requires heightened awareness, and the world of ontology requires spiritual awakening. Ontology is a metaphysical dimension of 'being'. Management focuses on the process of 'doing' and obtaining 'results'.

> 66
>
> Spirituality through mythology focuses on one's 'being' rather than just 'doing'. It is the shift from 'being', in which the process, the 'doing' gets purified. Actions that emerge from such purification lead not only to profit, but also to profitable growth. 99

Reflect on this story.

There once lived a great mathematician in a village outside Ujjain. He was often called by the local king for advice on matters related to the economy. His reputation had spread far and wide. So it hurt him very much when the rich village headman told him, "You may be a great mathematician who advises the king on economic matters, but your son does not know the value of gold or silver."

The mathematician summoned his son and asked him, "Which is more valuable – gold or silver?"

"Gold," said the son.

"That's right. Why then does the village headman make fun of you? Why does he claim that you don't know the value of gold or silver? He teases me every day. He mocks at me in front of other village elders, calling me a father who neglects his son. This hurts me. I feel everyone in the village is laughing behind me, because you do not know which is more valuable, gold or silver. Can you decipher this for me, son?"

So the mathematician's son told him as to why the village headman carried this impression. "Every day, on my way to school, the village headman calls me to his house. There, in front of all village elders, he holds out a silver coin in one hand and a gold coin in other. He asks me to pick up the more valuable coin. I pick the silver coin. He laughs, the elders jeer, and everyone makes fun of me. Everyone around specially derives pleasure in seeing me as a fool. And then, I go to school. This happens every day. That's how they tell you, I do not know the value of gold or silver."

The father was confused. His son knew the value of gold and silver, and yet when asked to choose between a gold coin and silver coin he always picked the silver coin. "Why don't you pick up the gold coin?" he asked. In response, the son took the father to his room and showed him a box. In the box were at least a hundred silver coins. Turning to his father, the mathematician's son said, "The day I pick up the gold coin the game will stop. They will stop having fun and I will stop making money."

Sometimes in life, you have to play the fool because your seniors and your peers, and sometimes even your juniors like it. That does not mean you lose in the game of life. It just means allowing others to win in one arena of the game, while you win in another. You have to choose which arena matters to you and which does not.

Reflection Point

Recount a half-truth situation in your life... and recall which side you are looking at. Is it the fact or the narrative that you built around it?

Are you factually seeing that happiness is not in the world of objects or is it that you are conceptually accepting that happiness is not in the world of objects?

The World of People
– Mirroring Oneself

The second dimension is the 'world of people'. With people, do not be mathematical. Do not use the same yardstick. It is a sad thing that people start relating to people with a view to making use of them. In mythology, what gets highlighted very emphatically is that you should not be utility-oriented in relating to the world of people, a world with which you have to constantly relate.

You should be musical in relating to people. And the greatest piece of music is 'love'. There is no music which is more melodious than love. To the world of people be musical, in the sense that you should relate out of love.

When you start relating out of love, you will never use people. You will respect them.

> " Look closely: people love objects and use people, instead of using objects and loving people. That is the problem. "

Mythology offers a possibility for one's journey, to move from liking to loving and from loving to devotion. A dedicated approach to devotion, brings transformation.

If there is no love in your relationship to the world of people, then you start controlling people, dominating them, playing power games and indulging in power struggles.

The tale of two characters from Mahabharata amply demonstrates this.

In the entire Mahabharata, Dhritarashtra lived his life craving for retaining the throne with his family. He was always after the throne; his frustration and greed led to the fall of the dynasty. Vidura, suggested that their brother Pandu be made the king, as Dhritarashtra was blind. Dhritarashtra sensed the throne slipping from his hands and he was resentful. He initially ceded the crown, but this resulted in it being protected for him to regain it, later in life.

Further, his lust for power compelled him to choose his son as the king, even after he was found unworthy. He favoured his eldest son Duryodhana to be his heir.

Dhritarashtra proved that his blindness was not limited to his physique. He was blind in his mind too. He was blinded by the love for his son. He couldn't see the evil nature of his son which was gradually growing. He was so blind in his love for his son that he remained silent even as his son reached new heights of notoriety. It was not only Duryodhana, but all his sons (except Yuyutsu) that were evil natured. He, being a father, had failed in his duty to guide them to the right path. His blind love and silence over his sons' misdeeds encouraged them to continue in their misguided ways.

Dhritarashtra did not intervene when Draupadi was being disrobed. However, when Draupadi was about to curse the Kuru dynasty, Dhritarashtra and Gandhari were quick to ask her not to curse them.

In the entire Mahabharata, Dhritarashtra never advised his son to walk on the path of dharma. It was his indecisiveness in guiding his son that led to the Mahabharata war. It was only when the Pandavas emerged victorious and all his sons were slain by Bhima, that he found time to act and decided to take revenge for the death of his evil sons. He tried to crush Bhima with his bare hands, but thanks to Lord Krishna who switched Bhima with an iron statue, nothing untoward happened.

Dhritarashtra is an example of one who lacked the will to stand up for good causes.

Secondly, his son Duryodhana, the Kuru prince, was the most corrupt and morally disgraceful. An understanding of Duryodhana's character will lead to the necessary understanding of the psyche's dark side. Such holistic understanding will bring one closer to achieving self-actualisation.

Duryodhana represents all the negative characteristics not present in the Pandavas' nature, and he is also the poster boy of the Kurus, being Dhritarashtra's first son. Duryodhana's behaviour reflects of immorality. He is blinded by jealousy and greed for the Pandavas' wealth and good fortune. He is easily prejudiced against them and holds deep grudges. Hence, he is the epitome of 'what one ought not to be'.

A World of Your own Self

In this world, learn to be meditative. The more meditative you are, the more would you start experiencing the deeper layer of your own self. You will find that there are different layers to you: *sthoola shareeram,* or gross body, *sooskhma shareeram* or subtle body, *karana shareeram* or causal body, and then, pure *sakshi chaitanya or* the witnessing consciousness.

You have a body and you take the body to be yourself. This physical body is the *sthoola shareeram.* Your mind and intellect, the subtle body, is called the *sooskhma shareeram.* If you go beyond the mind and delve deeper still, there is what is called the *karana shareeram*, a sheath of ignorance. At the deepest level, beyond the body, the mind (and intellect) and the sheath of ignorance, is pure awareness. This pure awareness is called *sakshi chaitanya.*

To discover and realise this 'pure awareness', you must be meditative. Otherwise, you will find you are bound and shackled in this life. The more meditative you are, the more liberated your life will be. As you delve into yourself, you will discover that your fears are purely imaginary.

The more you start enquiring, the greater is the possibility for difficulties and delusions to disappear. The only problem is that most of the times you do not know how to look at things. The art of seeing is a state of meditation. As you delve into the deeper layers of the self, you have to pass through certain doors – the door of the body, that of the mind and, of the ignorance that surrounds you.

Very few of you really go deeper into the domain of your mind. So many cobwebs are created due to this lack of enquiry. And these cobwebs can make a person really unhappy. When you are anchored in the structure of the mind, however much you get your desires, there are always better things for you to desire. If your happiness is based on a desiring mind, life will always be unhappy. You must go beyond the mind - otherwise you will find greed taking over. The greedy mind will go on and on demand for more. When you start becoming aware, you will experience all these nuances.

Therefore, to be meditative is to be aware of your body, mind and ignorance.

Can the 'desiring mind' transform itself into an 'abiding' and 'receptive mind'?

Ontologically, you can 'refine or optimise an experience' or else you will 'minimise experience' and thus miss alacrity in life.

Reflect on this incident.

Prior to the commencement of the Mahabharata war, Lord Krishna asked all warriors as to how many days would it take, if each of them were to finish the war by themselves i.e. as lone warriors. Bhishma replied that it would take him 20 days. Dronacharya said that he would take 25 days. Karna said that it would take him 24 days and Arjuna said that it would take him 28 days. Barbarik, however, astonished Lord Krishna with his answer. He said it would take him not more than a minute to win the battle by himself. The story unfolds in the following manner:-

Barbarik was the son of Ghatotkach and the grandson of Bheema. Having learnt the art of war from his mother, Maurvi, he was a brave warrior even in his childhood. He wanted to attain Moksha in the shortest possible way and was advised by his mother that it was only possible if he encountered Lord Krishna Himself in a combat.

He meditated deeply. Pleased with his meditation, Lord Shiva awarded him with three powerful arrows.

The first arrow would mark his enemy with a red dye. The second arrow would mark the things that he wanted to save. The third arrow would destroy the enemy target marked with red dye in the first step or destroy everything not marked, in the second step.

Barbarik's Guru however asked him to swear, by way of an assurance as guru-dakshina that Barbarik wouldn't use the arrows for his personal vengeance.

Lord Krishna wanted to test the powers of Barbarik. Thereby, he went to meet him in the guise of a Brahmin and requested him for a demonstration of his arrows.

He asked Barbarik to demonstrate his powers on a tree. He asked him to treat each leaf of the tree as his enemy and make a hole through them.

Barbarik started meditating. While he was meditating, Lord Krishna plucked a leaf from the tree and hid it under his own feet.

The first arrow was shot and it marked all the leaves in a red dye and started rotating around Lord Krishna's feet. Lord Krishna was shocked, but realised that there was nothing that could possibly stop the infallible powers of Barbarik and revealed His true self.

Lord Krishna then enquired Barbarik as to which side was he planning to fight for, in the Mahabharata war. Barbarik expressed his desire to fight for the Kauravas as Lord Krishna would be on the other side with the Pandavas. When asked why so, he stated that in order to reach salvation or moksha in the shortest time, it was possible only by fighting against Lord Krishna Himself in the war. Lord Krishna then revealed the paradox of Barbarik's impossible mission. As the potential of the three arrows made him the most powerful warrior on the battlefield, and to save the Pandavas, Lord Krishna asked for Barbarik's head. Barbarik readily accepted to Lord Krishna's demand. Pleased with his devotion, Lord Krishna granted him a boon.

Barbarik expressed his desire to witness the epic battle of Mahabharata. Lord Krishna promised him that even with his head severed from the body, he would continue to be in a conscious state. His head would be placed on a hill overlooking the battlefield, and he would be able to witness the whole war.

Barbarik, being a true warrior and disciple of Lord Krishna, readily agreed and severed his own head.

At the end of the war, the Pandavas argued amongst themselves as to who has to be credited for their victory. Lord Krishna suggested that Barbarik should be allowed to make that decision as he was a neutral witness to the whole war. At this, Barbarik concluded that it was Lord Krishna alone who was responsible for the Pandavas' victory: His advice, presence of mind and game plan were most crucial. Every arrow shot at the Pandavas, was countered by the presence of Lord Krishna's famous disc.

In his short life, Barbarik made a wise choice.

Reflection Point

Is the message of this chapter fully internalised, imbibed and assimilated?

What have you done to internalise, imbibe and assimilate this message?

Jealousy has its own logic. Have you observed jealousy operating in your life with sharpness as deep as possible for you?

The Transcendental Leader
– Ontological Paradigm

A leader is a visionary that inspires her team, guiding, assisting and facilitating where necessary, to drive an enterprise towards success and profitable growth. Leaders go beyond the nuts and bolts of accomplishing tasks or managing a team. They are dreamers, thinkers, catalysts of change and much more. And, they come in different types, with their own strengths and weaknesses.

The Mahabharata, one of the greatest epics, gives us many great leaders. Spiritualists speak of Lord Krishna as the greatest of them all. This is perhaps because the great Lord brings a dimension to leadership that goes beyond success in the material world. By setting an example, He guides us to success that transcends to the spiritual realm. He shows us the polarities that are at war within all of us: the Ego and the Self.

Ontological leadership is a spiritual dimension, stemming from the metaphysics of 'being'. Indian ethos highlight that one's centre of being should be based on the macro of five elements which are reflected in one's physical form. The five elements are — air, space, fire, water and earth.

If one's centre of 'being' is anchored in space, it is a sign of being open and one has the potential of being as vast as the sky.

The quality of air is the ability to touch everything and move on; this tells us that a leader should not stick to a particular experience.

If we closely observe, fire is not attached to anything. It burns both garbage and diamond. The leadership quality that is implicit in this is – do not be attached but be committed.

Water has the quality of being flexible and flowing. Hence, a leader can learn to be both free-flowing and flexible in approach while dealing with people and situations.

Earth represents the very ground of all beings and it denotes a deep sense of acceptance. It bears both, the neem tree as well as the rose plant, with equal ease. A leader can learn a great lesson by just observing the earth.

Therefore, the centre of ontological leadership emerges from the qualities of the five elements, enumerated above.

So let's look at leadership in the material realm of the corporate paradigm and, through this understanding of how to achieve success, move towards the ultimate victory in the spiritual paradigm.

A CEO of a company in one of the interactions asked me, "There are various people that we consider as leaders. Can you broadly classify them?"

Research shows that leaders can be broadly classified into four main types:

◆   Strategic
◆   Directive
◆   Team Building
◆   Operational

Strategic leaders are reality-analysts. Objectivity and rational thought are very important, for them. They ask hard questions and are ready to put vision above people. They take pride in their knowledge, aspire to find the right key to wisdom and often stay in the background. But their focus is on facts rather than emotions and can give the impression of being 'robotic'. Decision-making, is time-consuming for them, as they tend to lean towards perfection.

Directive leaders weave the big picture. They paint broad strokes and don't like to spend much time in the process details. As effective speakers, they have a high motivational capacity and possess the ability to make people feel important. They are great, in dealing with large groups and direct them to a set goal, but not so with individuals. A short attention span with restlessness means that they might be acting, ignoring financial limitations.

Team building leaders are all about people. They're charismatic and enjoy rallying people around a common cause. Their knack for generating high morale receives loyalty and respect from people. But they can also be hurt by people, allowing relationships to hinder progress. This means that sometimes, they tend to ignore agendas and action plans.

Operational leaders are very practical. Devising systems and processes to run things smoothly comes easily to them. So, they bring a lot of stability from their leadership. They can create new solutions to old problems. But they dislike conflict and sometimes fail to see the big picture; a shortcoming which can make them slip into 'managing' rather than 'leading'.

Whatever type of leader you are, however, certain characteristics lie at the roots of success. Lord Krishna teaches us what these are. Let us examine a few.

How does one achieve Spiritual Leadership Qualities?

Know Yourself

This is the key to becoming a great leader. Which of these five leadership traits best describe your qualities as a leader?

◆ Knowing your strengths and weaknesses.

◆ Transforming weaknesses into learning lessons.

◆ Strengthening the strengths.

◆ Knowing your hidden potential in areas other than your functional strengths.

◆ Seeing yourself as a possibility thinker rather than one who merely operates on quick fixes.

Knowing yourself means going beyond understanding personality traits. There is something in you that is transcendental, profound and eternal. Can you see this? The nature of this 'self' is eternal. It is filled with love. The 'self' sees all beings as an extension of the great and Supreme Being. It understands the interconnectedness of things. Therefore, when you lead with the sacred 'self', you will see the connection between the vision that drives you as a leader and the resources in hand that can efficiently realise that vision.

Going one step further, the 'self' also understands the meaning of true 'success'. It is not just about the highest profitability or the greatest breakthrough in knowledge. It is not about the clothes, cars or large mansions. Such achievements are gone in the blink of an eye when compared to the eternity of existence. Therefore, success, the 'self' knows, is the realisation of that Supreme Love, from which 'maya' or illusion veils us. The 'self' knows of its connection to the 'Supreme Being'. Your achievements, your profitability and your growth, whether individually or as an enterprise, is therefore not your own, but really the benediction of the Supreme.

Lord Krishna, therefore, tells us to place success where it belongs – as a polarity of failure. Great leaders around the world discern this. They know that failure can teach many lessons, and use it as an opportunity for growth. When Steve Jobs was fired by the board of directors of Apple, he came back stronger and better than ever, going on to reinvent the company's image and making it one of the most profitable in the world.

Be Detached

When you learn to place success and failure as mere inter-linked polarities, when you are open to both success and failure, such openness makes you go beyond success and failure, thus you would transcend both. Such transcendence brings detachment: *whether I succeed or fail, I must do my duty*. Detachment brings with it, objectivity. This is crucial when taking tough decisions in the corporate world. Detachment helps you see the bigger picture, uncoloured by personal sentiment.

नटाङ्गनान्यायः

The maxim of "a hero and heroine."

Relates to the conversation between a hero and a heroine on a theatrical stage. The hero asks the heroine as to whose wife she is. She replies that she's his wife. Implies that the theatrical relationships are false, their usefulness leading only to a temporary and bemusing effect. Man's life too is a theatre stage and, its connectedness with others in various relationships is therefore nothing but an illusory.

It is the ego which claims all to itself. It creates an identity called 'I' veiling your true 'self'. This 'I' creates the illusion of an existence separate from the Supreme Being. And it claims all actions, both success and failure, for itself. That means it attaches a setback in the workplace to your very nature, taking away your self-worth when you fail to finish a task or meet a deadline. Similarly, it attaches success to your nature, telling you, that you are worth something because you accomplished what you set out to do. So it tells you, you are worthless when you fail and wonderful when you succeed. Thus, the ego attracts unhappiness and colours your world views.

This 'I' creates boundaries. It takes you away from the interconnectedness of all things. It fails to see the inherent strength and beauty within all beings and wants to 'be the best' at everything. While a competitive spirit is a good thing, ruthless competition can destroy a team. Great leaders unite resources and talent. They do not divide out of fear of being replaced in their jobs.

Nurture People

When you begin to see all people as extensions of the Supreme Being, and thus, connected to you, you will learn to recognise the power and potential of those you lead. Duryodhana failed to realise this. In the Mahabharata, Lord Krishna gave an option to both Arjuna and Duryodhana – *do you want me or my armies?* Arjuna chose the great Lord, while Duryodhana chose His armies. Arjuna knew the power of the Lord and His wisdom. Ultimately, this is what won the war.

Yet another example from the Mahabharata can be of relevance here:

> Kunti, the mother of Pandavas shares her plight with Vidura, the Prime Minister of Hastinapur. She mentions the dichotomy that she faces, her heart as a mother cries out in agony when her son Karna whips himself as suta putra (son of a charioteer). Being repeatedly humiliated on the status of his birth, by the society, though the truth was otherwise, she shares that she's unable to openly declare Karna as her son, a Kshatriya.

> Vidura replies compassionately, "Though I am born as dasi putra

(son of a maid), never once have I whipped myself on that score. I am grateful for the duty assigned to me and able to do it wholeheartedly... it is not the paristiti (situations) of life, but instead, the manostiti (state of mind) that one should really reflect on."

These words soothe the despairing heart of Kunti.

The three-fold qualities that one can imbibe from the life of Lord Krishna are:

Ananda Lahari (waves of joy)*, Prema Lahari* (waves of love) and *Soundarya Lahari* (waves of beauty).

Let us examine how these can be applied in the domain of leadership.

Ananda Lahari: A leader learning to enjoy the process, enjoys the difficulties while reaching the goal and yet orients people towards the set goal and more importantly, allows them to enjoy the fruits when the goal is reached.

Prema Lahari: A leader learning not to operate from likes and dislikes thereby getting trapped in 'positionality', but bringing forth love as a fragrance of his soul in a team, irrespective of who receives it.

Soundarya Lahari: A leader learning to see beauty in 'what is' and directing the team to cosmic beauty which includes the whole.

Thus, a leader possessing above qualities creates leadership that makes others wiser as a result of love and commitment. Such a leader also ensures that the impact of leadership lasts even in her absence with a rejuvenating presence for her team.

Team Work and Management

A director in a multinational company came to one of our monthly meets and in a confused state narrated how he had many talented people in his group but he was hardly able to get the best from them. What was the solution?

The best example that comes to my mind is the team and unity among the five Pandava brothers, from an episode of the Mahabharata.

In the Mahabharata, the protagonists were the Pandavas. Each of the five brothers represented a particular heroic trait. For example, Yudhisthira demonstrated leadership and dharma; Bhima characterised strength and fearlessness; Arjuna was the face of patience and compassion; Sahadeva was wisdom and beauty and Nakula was the most handsome. That the brothers were at their strongest when together, was due to the fact that they were each predominated by a particular and admirable characteristic.

Together, they reinforced each other, forming an almost invincible group. Yet they were weak when working individually. For example, Yudhisthira lost the kingdom and, very nearly, his wife too, in the dice game with Duryodhana. He allowed the stakes to rise higher and higher until he and his brothers had nothing left.

Each Pandava brother had his own strength and weakness.

What one can learn from them is – their strengths were united. Their weaknesses were in the background, backed by a factor called 'the grace' of Lord Krishna.

Steps for Better Team Work

It is easy to bring people together for accomplishing objectives. It is, however, far more difficult to create the bonding that transforms a group of individuals to an effective team.

There are several steps you can take to improve your teamwork and management skills. The first of these is learning to have an overview of your team's good.

नष्टाश्वदग्धरथन्यायः

The maxim of "the destroyed carriage and horse."

Taken from the story that one day two people set out in their respective horse driven carriages. On the way, their carriages accidentally caught fire. Resultantly, the carriage of one and the horse of the other, were destroyed.

However, through mutual consent they got one carriage ready with what remained of their carriages and they returned home by that carriage. This tells us that by through unified efforts, we can fulfil our individual wants. "Union is strength".

Think of Your Team First

Good teamwork is the result of synergy between all team members, governed by a strong sense of unity and togetherness. There is no iota of an 'I' in the team, as it is said. An individual is a part of the larger whole and, his or her actions will affect that larger whole. A team member, therefore, must have an adjusting and flexible attitude with the willingness to set aside personal whims, for the greater good of the team. This, essentially, is the setting aside of the ego, with its endless personal desires, and requires a certain selflessness.

Simple steps to set aside the ego in teamwork could be as follows:

◆ Imbibe a vibrant value that the team is more important than the individual.

◆ Such a value must be in continuous communication mode in a team.

◆ A deep-rooted belief that system is above the individual, and learning to respect the system.

- Profess the value of what 'I can give' rather than 'what I can take' from the team.

- To operate from a focus to enhance strengths and to put aside weaknesses, as an individual's weakness, likes, dislikes, preferences, demands and idiosyncrasies weaken the team.

Praveen is part of a three-member team working on innovative solutions to a company's technology challenges. A quiet and shy person by nature, he finds it difficult to express his views in the open. Lately, he has noticed that his other two team members have been discussing ideas and sharing plans without his knowledge. He feels left out and lost because though he is shy by nature, Praveen knows he can make valuable contributions to the team. However, he feels constantly overwhelmed in team discussions.

What is the key to a good discussion?

Discussion Tips

If a person is shy, he must understand that his shyness is 'his problem', and not that of the team. The nature of shyness is that it is caught in a structure of 'looking good' rather than 'being good'. He must learn to put aside 'looking good' rather than feeling good. This 'looking good' is the result of the ego presiding over everything else. This ego can also interpret a situation without his knowledge. Once this happens – what is not factual, appears as factual. In Indian spirituality, it is termed as 'Maya'. 'Ya' 'Ma' as 'Maya' that which is 'not, appears to be'.

Consider this more deeply. Their discussion without Praveen's knowledge may also be an act of their spontaneity and not intentional. Maybe because of a complex nature that Praveen often projects, they may be talking without his knowledge.

Even if so, so what? Adi Shankara has written a poem in which he asks, 'tatkim...' So what? It is the ego which dictates that he should be involved. Either way, he need not be hurt. He must understand that in a team, everyone need not know everything.

For example, in the armed forces, what the General thinks, is not necessarily known to a soldier, as the army functions as a team.

Each one shares with another, based on one's comfort zone. Understand this. Also note that if the comfort zone becomes addictive, that's a problem too. Be awake to such a dimension. Lord Shiva says, '*Jnanam Jagrathaha*'. Understanding one's knowledge is wakefulness.

अश्मलोष्टकार्पासन्यायः

The maxim of the stone and clay of earth.

A piece of clay from earth may be considered to be hard when compared with cotton, but it is soft when compared with a stone. All three substances are from earth. So a person may be considered to be very important when compared with his inferiors, but will sink into insignificance when compared with his seniors. This maxim is used to denote the relative importance of things in its own right.

How can you facilitate a safe atmosphere where even the shy members of a team feel they can speak out and voice their opinions?

It is the leader's responsibility to create a value that everyone's role in the team is important in the chain of events. The leader should be responsible for the following:-

Creating a Safe Space
All ideas generated in a team may not be good, while some of the ideas though not applicable in the present, can be useful later.

Leader's responsibility is to create value that each role is important in the chain of events.

There is an inspiring story from Ramayana.

Lord Rama's army, searching for Sita, reached the southern tip of the peninsula to cross over to Lanka. They travelled until they encountered a vast sea that they had to cross to reach Ravana's kingdom.

Lord Rama attempted to calm the raging ocean by shooting his magic arrows into the waves. But the King of the Sea rose up and said, "The seas cannot be overcome by force. Building a strong bridge is the only way out." So, Lord Rama ordered the monkeys to construct a stone bridge that could hold his entire invading army.

Monkey after monkey set to work carrying huge stones and enormous boulders to the seaside. Thousands of monkeys worked ceaselessly and Lord Rama was pleased. Then one of the monkeys noticed that a small brown squirrel rushed up and down from the hills to the shore carrying little pebbles in her mouth. "What is that little creature doing?" he wondered.

"What can you do in a huge task, move away," they said. "You are too small. You are not needed."

The little squirrel looked up and said, "I am helping to build the bridge to save Sita." All the monkeys began to laugh at the little squirrel. "We have never heard anything like this before," they said.

The squirrel answered, "I cannot carry rocks or stones. I can only lift small pebbles, but that is what I can do to help. My heart weeps for Sita and I want to be of assistance."

The monkeys moved the squirrel away, but she continued to carry small pebbles and pile them up nearby. Finally, one monkey lifted the little animal and threw her into the air. The squirrel cried out, "Rama!" The Lord lifted his hand and caught the squirrel safely in his palm.

It was just at that moment that the monkeys realised they needed the little pebbles to place between the larger stones to keep the bridge from falling.

Lord Rama said to them, "Dear monkeys, never despise the weak or the deeds of those that are not as strong as you. Each one serves according to one's strength and capacity, and each one is needed to make this bridge."

With three fingers, Lord Rama drew three stripes down the squirrel's back. "What truly matters is not the strength one has, but how great one's love and devotion is." From that day onwards, squirrels have had three pale stripes on their rich brown furry backs - marks of the great Lord Rama representing anugraha (grace) of Ishwara (the

Lord), Guru and Atma (self).
And that is how the strongest bridge across the sea was built.
"Each serves according to her strength."

How can you overcome shyness and personal difficulty while working with a team?

Work Peacefully – Avoid Conflict

Conflict is bound to occur when people are working together. Managing team members who disagree can be especially difficult if members are strong personalities unwilling to yield.

So, what lies at the core of peaceful teamwork?

How can you 'agree to disagree' respectfully and manage strong characters?

It is only by understanding that 'principles' are beyond 'personalities'. This has to be lovingly and yet firmly be addressed. Ultimately, the wellness of the organisation should be the guiding factor in such a situation.

Understand Your Team Members

Karan is required to manage a team of 15 individuals, each with a different style of working. There are some days when they produce great output and meet their objectives and there are others when they don't work well together at all. Hence, he is frustrated.

What does it take to understand another person so that you are able to work together harmoniously?

A leader should comprehend the dynamics of the team. All team members do not work with the same degree of efficiency on any given day. In a team some may be starters, some are doers, some are supporters, some are focused on figures, some are fun lovers, some are counsellors, some are finishers etc. A leader's hallmark is in his ability to organise them to function as an orchestra.

Give Constructive – not Destructive Criticism

Sooner or later something will go wrong. As the manager of a team, you will have to tell your team members what should change so that things improve. This is no easy task because criticism is never easy to give or to take.

How can you give constructive criticism without offending or hurting anyone's feelings?

Why is it difficult to take criticism of any kind? And how can we learn to take criticism better?

> " While giving constructive criticism, one must try not to label a person as wrong, but make him see the possibilities of what is right. Helping others to love what is right and at the same time being honest about what is incorrect, is the art of constructive criticism. "

Receiving Criticism

In the Bible, there is a saying- 'Hate the Sin, not the Sinner'. In fact, you must rejoice being pointed out for mistakes.

> " If one is hurt, one must rejoice at the discovery of the ego. If other's criticism is wrong, still one must rejoice seeing the other's non-clarity. "

The clarity that you should have – 'should be a clearing in others' as also yourself. And that is the role of clarity. Hence, it should be a 'clearing'. Either way, you should rejoice.

Lastly, even if you are hurt by other's criticism, you must learn not to hold hurt in a 'continuous mode', but in 'let-go' mode. Then you are a passage for hurt to come and go. This is spiritual growth. This is what Indian mythology offers in a mystical way.

There are many characters in mythology that teach you how to overcome hurt and criticism. Study them deeply.

Transparency

Miscommunication and confusion about task objectives often makes Vidya uneasy in her team. People in her team are constantly twisting each other's words to place blame on someone's shoulder. The result is that there is no transparency in anything happening within the team. Everything must be communicated by e-mail and even then, some are in the know of what's happening and some are not. People are fighting because there is confusion, instead of working together for a solution. This is creating chaos.

Why does transparency erode in a team? Why do people twist words and actions and play the blame game instead of owning responsibility for their actions? How can you make things more transparent?

People indulging in twisting and manipulating suffer from a psychological ailment dormant in them. These diseases bring out a complicated mind in an individual.

> A complicated mind cannot see life in a simple way. It 'majors' on minor things and 'minors' on major things.

Hence you find a complicated person complicates everything. Please study the life of Ravana and Duryodhana to amply understand these phenomena.

Lack of transparency is a sign of insecurity. Insecurity is a product of lack of 'sacred outlook'.

The complicated mind results when your inner energies are not harmonised. Your inner hurt is not healed. The patterns in you will mess up your perception. Thus, there is a need for inner cleansing. A person can live in heaven and create hell or vice-versa.

Have you seen people beg for a job in the corporate world? When the job is given, instead of enjoying their work, they mess up their lives through complications and create difficulties in others' life.

Reflection Point

Can you be a light unto yourself?

Is your outlook 'sacred' or 'insecure'?

On a scale of 1 to 10, what are your abilities to create a team?

Can you see dirty water though not fit for drinking, can put off a ravaging fire? Can you see such phenomena in your life?

Energy Management

One of the key questions in my CEO counselling program is from an MD of a company where thousands work under him and his main concern hovers around - how to manage high energy levels in the team.

In a world where hectic pace can increase stress and drain you, maintaining good energy level is important, not just for productivity but also for general well-being. So, what's energy, according to the Vedas?

The Vedas expound the understanding that all matter is, in fact, energy. The profundity of this principle is presently being validated through the tools of modern science. This confluence of Western science with Eastern knowledge manifested symbolically when Tesla met Swami Vivekananda, in the late 19th century. The electrical engineers among us will know about Tesla's significant contributions to modern science. These included the AC motor, as well as, power generation and transmission systems (1888), to list a few. After being introduced to Swami Vivekananda and hearing of Vedic teachings, Tesla was in awe of the profundity of this knowledge. He wished to bring out the relationship between energy and matter but had failed to do so. This was effectively presented to the world by Einstein. His paper on the theory of relativity showed to Western science what Eastern philosophy had known for more than 5,000 years. Let us examine this knowledge.

The laws of physics describe energy as that which is neither created nor destroyed but only changes from one form to another. Having, therefore, no beginning or end, energy is eternal. It is all pervading. Modern physicists discern that even matter is energy. Atoms, which make up the matter, are recognised today as constituting small vortices of energy that are constantly spinning and vibrating. If it were possible to focus on an atom through a powerful microscope, we would see small energy vortices called quarks and photons. If you focused even closer, you would see nothing at all. It would just be void. The atom has no physical structure. This makes all the material and physical world as we know it, a mere illusion.

In Sanskrit, energy is known as *Prana* or the primary energy. However, the understanding of *Prana* takes us beyond the Western scientific concept of energy.

It has 'many levels' of meaning from breath to the energy of consciousness itself. *Prana* is not only the basic life-force, it is the master form of all energy working on the level of mind, life and body. Indeed, the entire universe is a manifestation of *Prana*, which is the original creative power.

How can you manage your energy to stay active throughout the day and increase productivity?

Firstly understand in detail how to manage the five *koshas*, as explained in the section *Uncovering Your True Self*.

Study the chapter in detail *Ashtanga Yoga* in the coming section which dwells on the eight limbs of yoga as opposed to the standard comprehension that yoga is all about certain postures.

Observe the play of energies in a family or an organisation as a discipline and make effort to change it when needed. Convert rigid energies into a free-flowing, all-inclusive energy.

Be aware of intellectual appreciation, and at the same time, emotionally rejoice in the play of energies.

As a leader, sheer intellectual appreciation of 'energies' is incomplete. A leader should create inspiring and unifying 'energies' which should be productive.This flexibility involves alertness resulting in pliability.

More importantly, a leader should emotionally rejoice in the creation as part of enhancing her emotional quotient.

Also be aware of the team that just emotionally rejoices but intellectually does not participate. Sheer emotional rejoicing without intellectual acumen is incomplete and hence blocks team building. Therefore, a leader intelligently harmonises intelligence quotient, emotional quotient and spiritual quotient of energies at work.

Also watch out for elements that create obstacles, pseudo-intellectual appreciation and pseudo-emotional appreciation. It is a well-known fact that group energies quickly get influenced and the result... both positive and negative rubs on to the team.

Here is an example from Mahabharata that illustrates energy management. There's a profound message in it, worth pondering.

In the war of Mahabharata, the fall of Bhishma affects Karna. He meets the god-like great man, lying on his deathbed, with his eyes closed! Overcome with emotion the teary-eyed Karna speaks, 'Oh, Pitamahah, Kurushreshta! It is Radheya! The man you hated, for no fault of mine, as soon as you set your eyes on me.'

Bhishma hears him, opens his eyes with difficulty and looks at Karna. He then sends his attendants away, with an embracing love welcomes Karna.

'Come, my dear opponent, if you had not come to visit me now, it would not have been praiseworthy. You are not a Radheya, you are a Kaunteya. I have no hatred for you, my child. I spoke to you harshly only to bring down your ego and pride. I feel that you hate Pandavas for no reason. It is the reason why I spoke to you harshly. I am aware of your great courage and your limitless generosity. You are like a god. There are not many like you. You are equal to Arjuna in your ability. There is no anger in me now. Man cannot go against the will of God. Pandavas are your brothers. If you want to make me happy, go and join your brothers. Let the enmity die with me; let all the kings live happily.

Karna replies, 'Grandfather, I know that I am a Kaunteya, son of Kunti. But when Kunti did not want me and let go of me, a charioteer brought me up! Duryodhana recognised my worth. I cannot turn these facts into lies. I have pledged my body, my wealth, my reputation and everything else to Duryodhana. What is required to be done cannot be changed by anyone. Who can change God's will? It is time for destruction of the world. You have seen signs of this, and also spoke about it in the royal court.

'I know that the Pandavas and Lord Krishna are invincible, but, I am enthused to fight them. If you give your consent with love and

affection, I believe I can fight them. If I have spoken ill of you out of anger or misbehaved, please forgive me.'

Bhishma replies, 'Karna! If you are unable to control your intense enmity, I consent! Give up your anger and sorrow and perform the duties of a warrior well and achieve a happy state of mind. Try your best to be virtuous; your wishes will come true. Depend on your strengths and bravery, forsake arrogance. There is no better dharma for a kshatriya than to fight a war. I tried my best for peace, but could not succeed. The victory belongs to those who are on the side of dharma.' Karna salutes Bhishma and leaves.

Bhishma understood that he was supporting adharma even though he had a deep-rooted value for dharma. He was trapped by his vow to protect Hastinapur.

Karna also knew that he was siding with adharma though he valued dharma, greatly valued dana (charity), and yet, he ended up supporting adharma.

Each one was reflecting the others' folly inspite of seeing value in being good. In the above conversation, there is an intuitive understanding that created 'inner clearing' inspite of their individual entrapments.

Finally, the two ill-starred men, grandfather and grandson, met and managed a closure.

This is one rare example of a life-long perception that was transformed through the inter-play of energies in a single conversation.

Further, Lord Krishna through his life, demonstrates the role model of a leader – ideal for intellectual creation, rejoicing emotionally, supporting the energy field in a group and lifting the energy level when facing a demanding situation in Mahabharata. Reflect on how he handled others' energies.

Wasn't Lord Krishna's life one of understanding a given situation, firm in the resolve to deal with it with necessary energies, being flexible in the approaches adopted, devising volatile strategy... yet, all based on the principle of goodness?

Can you be one such, to emulate?

Reflection Point

Is the essence of this chapter fully internalised, imbibed and assimilated to face the challenges of the modern day?

Reflect on the dialogue between Bhishma and Karna. Can you see each one mirroring the other and bringing forth healing energies? Can you apply this to a broken relationship and thus go beyond rigid perception?

Learning and Career Skills

One of my students, who has been fairly successful and leads a team in a fairly higher position, met me on a rainy day at my Ashram. He was seeking an answer to a question that bugged him – how to be on a learning curve to advance in his career and stay relevant? His performance appraisal was due the next day.

My response was as under:

Arun has been working in the same field of Information Technology for five years after his engineering graduation. While his pay package is good, he is struggling to direct his career in a way that gives him more satisfaction. How does he manage his career and skills to keep learning and also, be satisfied in life?

Learning is something that should happen throughout life. It should be an exploration of the world and circumstances in which you live, as well as a search for the true 'self'. Yet many among you stop learning, on the way. The best learning can come from observation.

Observe how thoughts manifest in you, how emotions work within you, how your private plays and self-dramas operate. There cannot be a better way to learn than observing yourself. Catch your inner voice. What does it say? Are you lost in your personal agendas or are you committed to transformation? All these observations need alertness. A great learning happens through them, rather than through mere books.

> "
> Hence the book of life should be the source for life.
> "

Difference Between Knowledge and Learning

'To know' is different from 'to understand'. To remember is not the true function of intelligence. With intelligence, you learn and grow but are unstructured. To learn involves unlearning and hence an important aspect of learning is being 'open'. In learning, you go on discovering. You are neither like a robot nor are you conclusive. Even if you conclude, you are open to a new dimension. Thus, a conclusion does not imprison you. In learning, you are receptive to truth. Learning is not based on memory, but on discovery. Life flows, it changes and if you are in a static conclusion, you miss life. Knowledge is conclusive but learning is a dynamic process of the discovery of one depth and another and so on.

Being trapped in knowledge, is a psychological limitation. Being without knowledge is like being rootless.

> "
> Understand that learning is like the wings, while knowledge is like the root. Both learning and knowledge should be in harmony. "

You should know what works and at the same time, you should be able to learn from other people. This harmony between knowledge and learning is known as the 'Mandala-Mystic' circle. Simply put, in the psychological world, it means that you should know your past and not get trapped by your past. And also, you should be open to the present and as well as the future. A wise blend of knowledge and learning with understanding is the mystic circle.

I read a piece a famous writer wrote:

Last year, I had a surgery and my gall bladder was removed. I was stuck to my bed due to this surgery for a long time.

The same year I turned 65 years of age and had to give up my favourite job. I had spent 30 years of my life in this publishing company.

That very year, I experienced sorrow at the death of my father.

That year, my son failed in his medical exams as he met with a car accident. He was in bed at the hospital with a cast on his limbs, for several days. The destruction of the car was another loss.

In the end, he wrote: Oh God! It was such a bad year!

When the writer's wife entered the room, she found her husband looking sad and lost in his thoughts. Standing behind him, she read what was written on the paper. She left the room silently and came back with another paper and placed it on side of her husband's writing.

When the writer saw this paper, he found his name written on it with following lines:

Last year I finally got rid of my gall bladder which had contributed to several years of a painful existence for me.

I turned 65 with sound health and retired from my job. Now I can utilise my time to write something better with more focus and peace.

The same year my father, aged 95 years, without depending on anyone or without being through any critical condition... met his Creator.

That very year, God blessed my son with a new life. My car was destroyed but my son stayed alive without suffering any permanent disability.

At the end she wrote: This was a year of immense blessing from God to me, and it passed well!

The writer was indeed happy and amazed at such beautiful and encouraging interpretation of the happenings in his life in that year!

In your daily lives, you must see that it is not happiness that makes you grateful but gratefulness that makes you happy.

How can you cultivate a learning attitude throughout life?

Continuing Arun's question, you'd see in the Vedas that there are two types of knowledge... *Paravidya* and *Aparavidya*.

Aparavidya deals with the world of objects and hence limited to the object of learning. *Paravidya* is also absolute learning where learning is about the self and truth. The exact knowledge of objects may lead you to success but not necessarily to fulfilment. On the other hand, *Paravidya,* provides fulfilment. One may have many successes in life but not fulfilment... that is Arun's problem. The very search for fulfilment is a spiritual search. Recognise it.

Reflection Point

Is there a prayerful pause, prayerful shock and prayerful direction from the above?

Have you learnt the art of re-framing an experience from the above example?

Risk and Change Management

"Are risk and change inevitable as the cogs of modern day management? Is there a way out or to what extent can one take risks in business?" A businessman in a family owned export house asked me this recently.

My reply was:

'It's not the strongest of the species that survives, nor the most intelligent that survives. It is the one that is the most adaptable to change.'

— Charles Darwin
English naturalist and author, 1809–1882

Change is inevitable. It comes with life and you should find ways to address it. While managing change at an individual level is definitely challenging, handling it at the organisational level, whether within a team of few, or across an enterprise of thousands, is even more daunting. It goes beyond adapting different processes or strategies. At its core, change in an organisation boils down to the people within it and how their approach to work differs from before. It is behaviour based and pertains to a shift in culture. Most importantly, it needs to be driven by a clear vision of what needs to be achieved. As with anything that requires the management of people, understanding and awareness are key aspects of change management.

Know Yourself. Know Your People. Know Your Business.
Change works best when initiated by the leaders. Unless the top management is seen to 'walk the talk', very little happens, in terms of real change.

How can you learn to know yourself better so that you can manage change more productively?

Change is a constant process.

◆ If you creatively address a change, you can profit from it.
◆ That in turn, would lead to higher productivity and enhanced quality.

You can learn from the ABCD technique in life. It means:–

A   Attitude to profit from change.

B   Belief in such a possibility.

C   Commitment to communicate constantly to yourself on the attitude to contribute and believe in those possibilities.

        Relegate complaints to the backyard so as to not dominate your lives.

D   Dare to go beyond what is comfortable and be adventurous. With this, you can manage change productively.

Leadership is giving your best to others and making them leaders. The joy of seeing others emerging as leaders is indeed a profitable growth. Else, team feels used and not inspired.

This is daring leadership.

> To know yourself better, you should be very observant to your thoughts, feelings, opinions etc. Observation without the interference of the observer is the magical key that you should discover within. Observe one's past. Past should be a reference point, not an imprisoning point.

Key Elements of Change Management

Communicate – the vision of what needs to be achieved should be clearly communicated. People also need to engage in this change process.

How can you learn to communicate better and engage people to change?

I'd suggest a simple process. It is called the 5 Fs'

Exercise being Fair, Friendly, Firm, Frank and Flexible in every communication.

Flexibility and openness in discussion are the key takeaways in an engaging relationship involving constant communication.

How can positive reinforcement help to manage changing the non-constructive voice of judgement?

Study the following diagram for the answer. Convert your inner vocabulary to take you towards the goal.

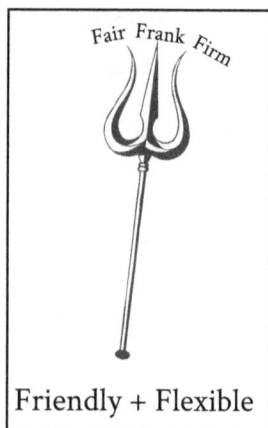

Fair Frank Firm

Friendly + Flexible

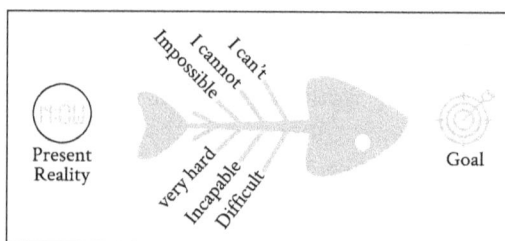

Present Reality — Impossible, I cannot, I can't, very hard, Incapable, Difficult — Goal

Risk Management

How can you build your inner resources to face and manage risk?

It is by using re-framing technique as discussed above.

नहि सुतीक्ष्णाऽपि असिधारा स्वयमेवोच्छेत्तुम् आहितव्यापारो भवति

The maxim of a keen sword.

It takes its origin from the fact that a sword, however, keen it may be, would not cut an object unless it is wielded by somebody.

It denotes that mere possession of a good thing produces no good, but there must be someone properly qualified to make good use of it.

Managing Risk

Manage risk with a deep understanding that one has of both, male energy as well as female energy within oneself. The concept of *Ardhanareshwara* from the Indian traditions makes it clear.

Both male and female energies in an individual are to be harmonised to create inner resources. For example, male energy thrives on insecurity while female energy seeks security. Both of these must be harmonised. This is the balance of *Yin and Yang, or Shiva and Parvathi*. The interplay of their energies creatively, is truly artistic.

With these as the internal organised energy resources, face the risk of life. However, the healthier approach would be to have a bucket plan in place that allows certain pockets of high risk, medium risk and low-risk activities.

If your male energy is too high, you will be uncomfortable with no risk and you will be addicted to meaningless achievement pursuits. If you have no male energy, you will not educate yourself to challenge or initiate high risk. A balanced being is one who opens his consciousness to all dimensions of risks... high risk, medium risk, low risk and no risk.

This is also applicable to money management of oneself, family or institution or organisation.

Here is the true story of risk-taking ability that should inspire everyone.

John Roebling was inspired by an idea to build a spectacular bridge connecting New York with the Long Island. However, bridge building experts throughout the world thought that this was an impossible feat and told Roebling to forget the idea. It just could not be done. It was not practical. It had never been done before.

Roebling could not ignore the vision of the bridge he had in his mind. He thought about it all the time and he knew deep in his heart that it could be done. He just had to share the dream with someone else.

After much discussion and persuasion, he managed to convince his son Washington, a budding engineer, that the bridge in fact, could be built.

Working together for the first time, the father and son developed concepts of how it could be accomplished and how the obstacles could be overcome. With great excitement and inspiration, and the headiness of a wild challenge before them, they hired their crew and began to build their dream bridge.

The project started well, but when it was only a few months underway, a tragic accident on the site took the life of John Roebling. Washington was injured and left with a certain amount of brain damage, which resulted in him not being able to walk or talk or even move.

Everyone had a negative comment to make and felt that the project should be scrapped since the Roeblings were the only ones who knew how the bridge could be built. In spite of his handicap, Washington was never discouraged and still had a burning desire to complete the bridge and his mind was still as sharp as ever.

He tried to inspire and pass on his enthusiasm to some of his friends, but they were too daunted by the task. As he lay on his bed in his hospital room, with the sunlight streaming through the windows, a gentle breeze blew the flimsy white curtains apart and he was able to see the sky and the tops of the trees outside for just a moment.

It seemed that there was a message for him not to give up. Suddenly an idea hit him. All he could do was move one finger and he decided to make the best use of it. By moving one finger, he slowly developed a code of communication with his wife.

He touched his wife's arm with that finger, indicating to her that he wanted her to call the engineers again. Then he used the same method of tapping her arm to tell the engineers what to do. It seemed foolish but the project was underway again.

For 13 years Washington tapped out his instructions with his finger on his wife's arm until the bridge was finally completed. Today the spectacular Brooklyn Bridge stands in all its glory as a tribute to the triumph of one man's resolute spirit and his determination not to be defeated by circumstances. It is also a tribute to the engineers and their teamwork, and to their faith in a man who was considered mad by half the world. It stands too as a tangible monument to the love and devotion to one's work.

One of the examples that we see from the Mahabharata war is –

The enigma of Lord Krishna choosing himself to be a charioteer – it is enigmatic higher consciousness taking a high risk by not choosing to fight the war, but ensuring victory in the process.

This is daring leadership.

Reflection Point

Will you be able to see a situation with special eyes to shed more light?

Can you apply the ABCD technique in your walks of life?

Can you be a possibility thinker?

Problem Solving

On a cold morning, during the meditation session, a recently promoted CFO, profusely sweating, and hazy in his thoughts, narrates an incident. While he solves one problem, yet another pops up. Problems — each one, is different from the other, and unique. More time and energy is spent, with him being on the continuous problem-solving mode. That leaves him with little time for productive work. What is the way out?

दण्डसर्पमरणन्यायः

The maxim of the stick and the serpent.

The maxim originates from good care to be taken in beating a serpent with a stick so that the serpent may be killed but at the same time the stick may not be broken, and it is used to denote that a clever man should conduct himself in such a way in performing a task that the object in view may be accomplished without any injury either to himself or to anybody else.

Actually Seeing the Problem

The first thing you must do is ask yourself whether you are seeing a problem factually, i.e., without imposing your perceptions on the problem. In seeing the problem 'as it is', lies the solution to the problem. Often times, your perception prevents you from seeing the problem, 'as it is'.

> You will understand that a problem appears exaggerated if you brood over it, especially with prejudiced and polluted patterns of thought and perception. If you set about solving it with clarity, you will be able to arrive at its solution.

Problems appear bigger than what they really are because you exaggerate them. When a problem is all that occupies your mind, it is natural for that problem to grow large enough to occupy all the available mental space.

The way your past creates perceptions, it clouds your present view of the things around you.

Develop the Right Thinking

Sometimes, we may have the right thought, but not the right thinking. Some of us think. Many of us think we think. Most of us never think of thinking. We don't even make a distinction between thought and thinking. There is an ocean of difference between thought and thinking.

Thought is static. It is an expression of your conclusions. It is an expression of your past. Thinking, on the other hand, is a dynamic process. Life too is a dynamic process. These two dynamic processes must meet. This would only happen if you are open to possibilities.

Learn to identify the thinking processes in your team.

Your intellect must teach you to be a part of the solution and not to be victims of problems. If you develop the intellectual will, you will find that your brain seeks solutions.

> "
> You have to treat problems as though they were exercise routines for the development of your mental faculties. Searching for a solution to a difficult problem has its own rewards. "

How can you develop right thinking?

Approach to the Problem

Most times, be it at work or home, one approaches a problem with a complaint and not with commitment. It is like a circle, the centre should be commitment and complaint should be the circumference, but very often, commitment is the circumference and complaint is the centre.

If you are alert, then you will operate with commitment rather than from complaint.

This alertness should have the quality of openness and in that space, you should confront a problem. Then you will not be a victim of the problem. Ineffective people approach a problem with worry, with anxiety, with fear, and that adds to the problem. But if you are alert to the problem, you must also be open to the problem. Then, in that alertness there is stillness, and in that stillness, your deeper intelligence flows.

It is said that during the fourteenth century, in South West Asia King Tamerlane's army suffered defeat. His army fled, in retreat. He was hiding when he noticed an ant trying to carry a grain of corn over the wall. It failed many times but finally succeeded. Fascinated by the scene, he was inspired by the fact that the ant, despite many failures, succeeded. He thus inspired his army and won the battle.

You can approach a problem wisely or foolishly. To approach a problem wisely, you must be open, alert and have fun with the problem. You must learn to enjoy the problem. You must learn to feel thrilled with the problem. If you enjoy the problem, then you will be bigger than the problem or else the problem will be bigger.

Reflect on the episode from Mahabharata.

Kalayavan was a powerful warrior who was undefeated in wars and combat. Kalayavan believed Lord Krishna was a powerful warrior. He attacked Dwarka. Kalayavan decided to challenge Lord Krishna to a duel. Lord Krishna strategically fled the battlefield. Lord Krishna lured Kalayavan into the cave where the great king of Treta Yuga, Muchukunda, was in deep slumber for thousands of years, after helping devas in an epic war with asuras.

Contemplating an absolutely undisturbed sleep, he was given a boon by Lord Indra that anyone who dared to disturb his sleep would get burnt to ashes immediately. Fast forward to Dwapara Yuga, in the darkness deep inside the cave, Lord Krishna covered Muchukunda with his shawl. Kalayavan assumed Muchukunda to be Lord Krishna, attacked him and thus disturbed his sleep. Kalayavan was immediately burnt and reduced to ash. Muchukunda, was delighted to see Lord Krishna too there, who was none other than Lord Vishnu. Lord Krishna advised him to perform austerity to cleanse his accumulated sins to attain Moksha (liberation).

After meeting the Lord, Muchukunda sets out of the cave. Muchukunda then performs a penance and finally achieves liberation.

Sometimes, a problem that is unique requires a unique solution. If one seeks a solution, the impossible is possible!

Problem Solving

When you start looking within, you develop extraordinary eyes. If you look at anything with such eyes, you will see the book of wisdom. That's what happened to the great sage Dattatreya, who it is said, had many gurus. When you examine all the gurus of Dattatreya, you will realise something: Dattatreya was able to look at life in a holistic way, unlike most of you. Therefore, by nature, a guru is holistic.

How does an ordinary person look at life? If you have a problem, you look at solving the problem through your likes, dislikes, your opinions and dogmas, your religious conditioning, your idiosyncrasies, your expectations, your fears, what you feel it should be etc. Dattatreya, however, solved the problems of life holistically.

An ordinary approach to problems is to be habituated to solving them in a particular way. All your problem solving is habitual, in the pattern. If you are habituated to a particular way of solving a problem, then you are imprisoned by that habit. When you are imprisoned, you are not free to look at the problem beyond the habit of your likes and dislikes and the way to solve it.

ऊष्ट्रकण्टकभक्षणन्यायः

The maxim of a camel and a thorny plant.

The camel likes much to eat the thorny leaves and bark of a certain plant though it has to suffer much pain. It is used to denote that one would be pleased to follow his own taste however inconvenient or undesirable it may in reality be.

So, are you free? You are bound by your own likes and habits. If so, are you really free? You are not free. A bound person binds himself further while solving a problem. To solve a problem, you should be free from habit. An inner freedom must be present. Only then you can look at the problem without the limitations of your likes and dislikes. When you can do that, and in that freedom... when you look at the problem, the very approach to the problem resolves the problem.

Sadly, very often your approach to the problem is very micro – small. And when this is the case, then that micro is bound by its micro – it limits you. Therefore, you can never really solve the problem.

How did Dattatreya approach the problems of life? He did so with an inner freedom. With that inner freedom, he looked at the sky, the wind, the python, the moth, the elephant, a lady pounding rice and many other such instances of life and was able to understand the human condition. He was so inwardly free, that in that freedom there was cognition. His mind was not bound by the shackles of his likes and dislikes.

Kalinga was a poisonous serpent living in the Yamuna river, in Vrindavan. The water of the Yamuna all around him boiled and bubbled with poison. No bird or beast could go near, and only one solitary Kadamba tree grew on the river bank.

The proper home of Kalinga was Ramanaka Dwipa, but he had been driven away from there by the fear of Garuda, the foe of all serpents. Garuda had been cursed by a yogi dwelling at Vrindavan so that he could not come to Vrindavan without meeting his death. Therefore Kalinga chose Vrindavan as his residence, knowing it was the only place where Garuda could not come.

Once, Lord Krishna and a few herd boys were playing. The ball they were playing with fell into the Yamuna river and Lord Krishna jumped after it. Kalinga rose up with his hundred and ten hoods vomiting poison. All the Gopis and people of Vrindavan came running towards the Yamuna bank as soon as they heard the news that Lord Krishna jumped into the river where the dangerous Kalinga was staying. Meanwhile, in the bottom of the river, Kalinga wrapped himself around Lord Krishna's body. Lord Krishna became so huge that Kalinga had to release him.

He immediately regained his original form, and when he saw that the Brij folk were scared of the serpent, he suddenly sprang onto Kalinga's head, and danced on the naga's heads. He started beating the serpent's heads with his feet, as he danced on them. Kalinga started vomiting blood and slowly began to die. But then the naga's wives came and prayed to Lord Krishna with joined palms, worshipping Lord Krishna and praying for mercy for their husband.

Kalinga, recognising the greatness of Lord Krishna, surrendered, promising he would not harass anybody. So Lord Krishna pardoned him and then let him go free. Lord Krishna asked Kalinga to leave the river and go to Ramanaka Dwipa.

The people who had gathered on the banks of Yamuna were terrified looking at the colour of water which was changing its hue to a poisonous shade. Gradually, Lord Krishna rose from the bottom of the lake, dancing on the head of Kalinga. When they saw Lord Krishna, everyone was happy and they broke into an ecstatic dance performance.

Reflect on this: How Ego becomes Self.

In the River of life, the ego like Kalinga creates unnecessary trouble. When the gopis (thoughts) rush to Lord Krishna (enlightened consciousness), Lord Krishna dives into the river and defeats it. This is called Kalinga Mardana.

When the death of the ego happens, the self survives like a snake not troubling others.

The root of all our problems is ego, not the self.

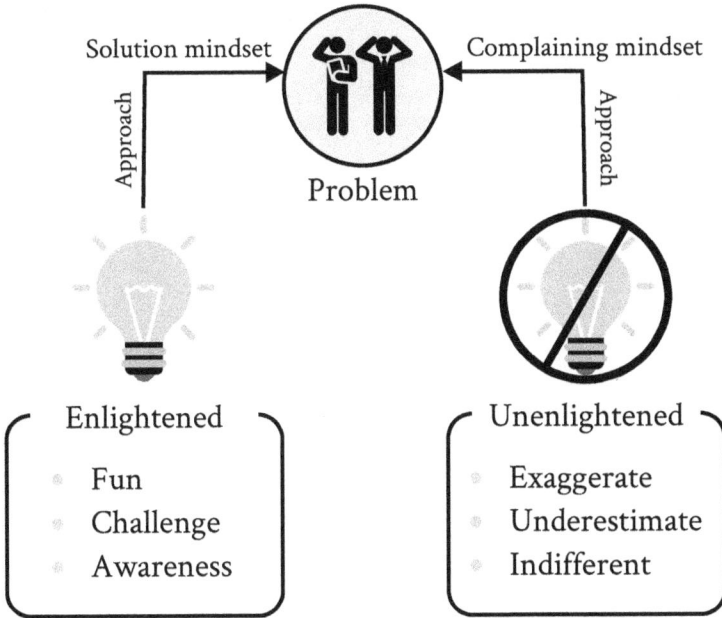

Enlightened

- Fun
- Challenge
- Awareness

Unenlightened

- Exaggerate
- Underestimate
- Indifferent

Reflection Point

Will you employ your spiritual key in a situation as above?

Dive into the river of your life and identify your Kalinga – the ego.

Inspect when you have a problem – Problem is not solved in the domain of the problem. The solution is found in the domain of the solution. Reflect on the episode of Kalayavan.

Conflict Resolution

How do you resolve conflict at work and at the same time continue enjoying working? This is the question from a Japanese delegate in my session at Indian School of Business.

My reply was through the following example.

Nandi and Bhringi are two of Lord Shiva's confidants that guard Parvati's palace. As the two confidants would never stop Lord Shiva at the gate, Parvati decides to have her own guard. She fashions a handsome son out of some clay from a pond and names him Ganesha.

On one occasion, when Parvati is at her bath, Lord Shiva turns up at the gate and is stopped there by Ganesha. He refuses to let Lord Shiva in, as per mother's instructions not to let anybody in.

Ganesha overdoes his duty by not allowing Lord Shiva into the palace. Lord Shiva tries his best to make little Ganesha see reason, but cannot. The rigidity between father and son leads to conflict. In the conflict that follows, Ganesha's head is severed.

Parvati laments over the tragic incident. Lord Shiva creatively transplants the head of an elephant and Ganesha is brought back to life.

Symbol of creativity is thus brought about in the form of Ganesha. He symbolises the harmony of the head of an animal and the body of a human and shows us that the principle of godliness exists in both.

> " Be alert to the fact that rigidity can lead one to devastation.
>
> Creative act happens through flexibility. "

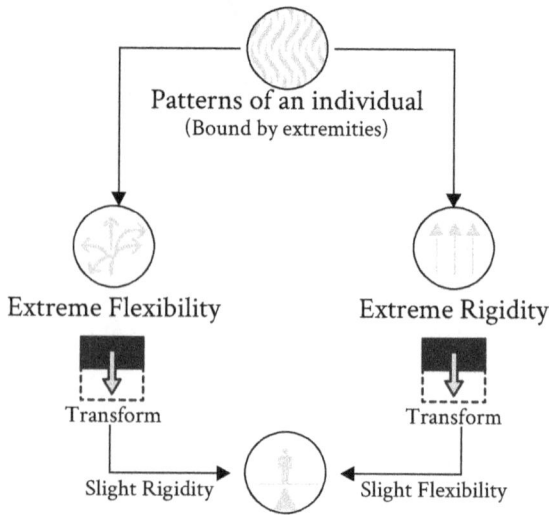

The lesson that can be learnt here is: Rigidity led to conflict between Lord Shiva and Ganesha. Over-addiction to duty is also a kind of disorder.

What's at the heart of that bitter dispute with your colleague? Is it just a personality clash or are there serious challenges to the way you work together?

> "
> Creativity is, therefore, a solution to resolve a conflict. This is the spiritual lesson. Please understand methodology in mythology. "

At surface level, it would appear that conflicts occur due to differences in opinions, approaches and beliefs. Avoiding them is impossible, especially in a professional setting. When a diverse group of people, each with their own mindset, come together to accomplish something, differences will occur. Suppressing or avoiding conversations about them, will only add or build pressure. It does not resolve anything.

Beyond surface level, conflict occurs from a deep need or desire – to be valued, understood, to feel secure and be fearless – not being met. It could also be a desire for greater closeness in working relationships.

So, what should you do in the face of conflict?

There are two things happening simultaneously at such times:

◆   the turmoil within;
◆   the conflict outside.

Observing Within

Be Aware – Manage Your Emotions

Almost the first reaction, in times of conflict, is that of anger. It is simplistic to say, 'Avoid anger completely.' Please remember, anger that is appropriate for the circumstance or situation, is a sign of intelligence. Disproportionate anger, on the contrary, is unintelligent.

Unfortunately, many of you indulge in disproportionate anger as you are not in sync with your feelings. Work pressure and stress leave you with little time to examine what you really need, or seek, in relationships, be it in the professional, or the personal arena. Not being aware of your deep-seated needs, you would not reflect on your own reactions. Anger seems to be the easiest way out, under such conditions.

Therefore, managing emotions boils down to understanding yourself and being aware, in the heat of the moment, as to what is transpiring within you, and why. Self-awareness forms the foundation for conflict management. It will help answer some fundamental questions:

Why am I really upset? Why did I react so strongly? How should I address that need? How should I manage myself through this process?

You should learn how to address these questions through careful self-examination.

How can you improve self-awareness and stay in touch with your feelings, so as to know what affects you, in times of conflict?

Be in Harmony With Conflict

Whether you initiate it, or you are at its receiving end, conflict causes stress. When conflict knocks your door, it is easy to feel overwhelmed and anxious.

However, it is possible to be in harmony with conflict and also with the fact that differences are inevitable. You can learn to dig deep into your inner reserves and work through difficult times or conversations. As mentioned, a strong foundation of self-knowledge and awareness is necessary for this. On top of that, is the ability to keep calm and quickly relieve any stress within you.

How can you keep calm and be in harmony, during times of conflict?

Reflecting Outside

Use Humour

No matter what happens in life, keep in mind that all things are temporary. Even the most challenging conflict will pass with time. Using humour that is apt for the situation or circumstances, can help ease resentment or frustration. It can even bring people closer, in conflicting situations. When there is humour, endorphins are produced in the body and this will make you feel good.

Lakshmi the goddess of fortune and Shanideva the deity of misfortune were once at loggerheads. They debated among themselves, as to who between the two, was better looking.

To resolve it, they approached Brahma, Shiva and Vishnu in that order. Each in this list, however, chose not to play judge, as the decision could spell doom for them. Vishnu in turn suggested that the duo approach sage Narada who'd be able to finalise this.

Narada could wriggle out of any tricky situation. Accordingly, the twosome met Narada to settle the issue.

Narada pondered over the tricky question. If he chose the goddess of fortune as better looking, he faced the dreaded wrath of Shanideva. On the other hand, proclaiming the opposite i.e., Shanideva as better looking, he stood to lose all his fortunes, including wisdom, forever.

He quickly worked a way out. He asked the contentious pair to do something like a ramp walk, in front of him. They obliged.

On completion, Narada gave his decision. He said, 'Going away from me, Shanideva looked good. And, while coming towards me, goddess Lakshmi looked good.'

The decision pleased both and Narada saved his day.

Compromise – Agree to Disagree

You don't always have to agree with what someone is saying or doing, but if you value a person's point of view, you can agree to disagree. In that state of respectful understanding, compromise is possible.

How to be more compromising?

Forgive and Let go

Abhishek remembers the day his colleague, Susheela, lost her temper on him because of a mistake in his work. Though they have talked over it, since then, he still feels resentment for her, for raising her voice, and also for some of the things she said. How can he really forgive and let go?

Forgiveness and letting go, is one of the most healing experiences, for any person. Yet most of you spend so much time keeping track of who upset you, and how you can hit back at them that you don't realise how much damage is being caused in the process. If a conflict is to be really resolved, there must be a sense of forgiveness and let go. 'Let go' is an art that cannot be taught, it has to be caught.

How to become more forgiving?

Let love communicate in a 'giving mode', rather than in a 'hurt mode'.

Abhishek, in order to let go, should not hold his hurt in a 'continuity mode'. Thus, he has to let go 'continuity mode' thought.

To forgive Susheela, he should be creative and bring forth an expansive heart so that he can be more humane to himself and his colleague.

Feel more than mere interpreting. Life, then becomes easier.

Effective Communication

Communication goes beyond just the words you speak. During conflict resolution, it is important to keep in mind that words are not the only means to convey your intent.

Non-verbal communication is also important. It's about facial expression, that one posture, touch and gestures. We will discuss this in greater detail in the section on communication skills.

A theory in the management illustrates a technique 80:20.

It means 80 percent of the result is obtained through 20% of the effort for effective productivity. This is able management. The converse is also true where very often in reputed institutions, 80% of effort and resources are spent to achieve 20% result.

What you can learn from this technique in conflict resolution is – if 80% is in worry and in narration, it will produce 20% result. But if 80% is in creating solution mode and only 20% in concern mode, such an equation makes it effective.

A constant scale to measure up on this equation would come handy.

Reflection Point

Are you bringing holistic self into play or caught in rigid opinion?

To be right is important or being happier is important... audit yourself.

Is your communication fair, friendly, frank, firm and flexible?

Creativity

A dean from a reputed university once asked me, "Swamiji, can one be constantly creative? How do I address such an issue with my research students? I have no clue. Is there more to it, from the Indian ethos point of view?"

What is creativity? Steve Jobs demystifies creativity, suggesting that it emerges in the context of ideas. Most of you often limit it to the realm of arts and the role of artists. Painters, musicians, dancers – they are the immediate association you have, for creativity. Yet, some of the greatest solutions in business and management spring from creative thinking. The corporate environment provides an outlet for creativity in the form of ideas, not just for the purposes of developing a tangible product, but even more so to address everyday challenges of enterprises. Creativity forms the base of any innovation. Thought leaders and managers today recognise this and work to develop a nurturing environment, for creativity to blossom.

Fostering Creativity

Deepak is part of a team that deals with process management. For nearly 3 days the team has been trying to solve a particularly challenging problem. Deepak has an idea, but he is too afraid to suggest it. What if it doesn't work and he may have to face the consequences?

Here, the role of managers is extremely important. Recognising and valuing ideas, helping employees overcome their fear of repercussions is also vitally important.

When you work as a team, you must be sensitive to increase the collective consciousness so that you can move away from the mechanical towards the creative. If you can do this, within yourself, you will not be ritualistic in life. Otherwise, life becomes a mere ritual, devoid of creativity. We have become machines in a mechanical world.

Control forms a very big part of that mechanical world. Everything is measured, monitored and evaluated for higher efficiency. Even spontaneity is scheduled. So where's the room for creativity in such a place? It is important to keep in mind that creativity is unlimited and unbounded. It cannot be measured or evaluated. Therefore, do not manage creativity, but rather, manage the 'creative process'.

> "
> Provide incentives and rewards and show that the creative process is both respected and rewarded.   "

Increasing Creativity From Within

Please reflect on the Muchukunda and Kalyavan episode narrated earlier where creativity is amply demonstrated by Lord Krishna to resolve a unique problem of a different age and time span.

> "
> From a spiritual angle, creativity happens when 'you are not'. Then the 'absence of you' is the presence of the creator and, the true creator is God. You are allowing the whole to function through you. Creativity belongs to the creator.   "

Even small acts like gardening, washing of dishes, cleaning the floor become a creative art, for you are allowing the whole to pass through you.

There is a Hasidic saying — 'When God gives, He does not give to you, but through you'.

In a spiritual paradigm, the peak of consciousness is – do what you love and love what you do, and then you are creative.

Look at Creativity Differently

It is not an act, but the quality that you bring to the activity. Your approach to what you are doing, walking, talking, etc. can be creative.

In another dimension, if you allow your thoughts not to be trapped in conclusions, opinions and thus get limited by them, but instead, allow 'thought to draw from the unlimited consciousness, from the whole, from the macro...' then, your thought becomes a beautiful instrument of creativity. And it results in action. Such an action is the function of the unlimited.

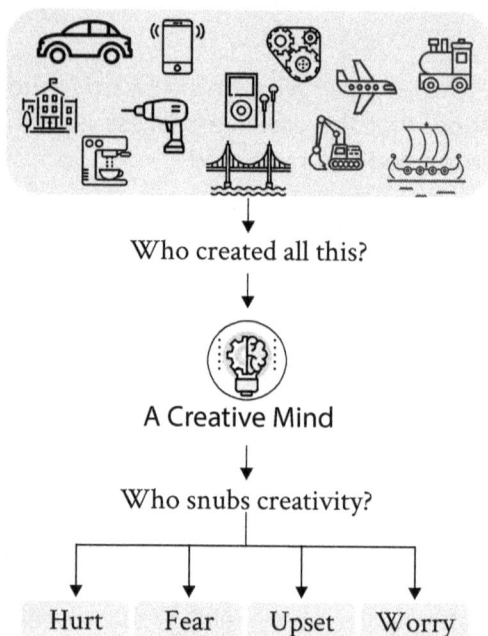

Who created all this?

A Creative Mind

Who snubs creativity?

Hurt   Fear   Upset   Worry

Reflect on this story.

Parijata, a tree that bore flowers with the most exquisite fragrance, was regarded to be the most beautiful in Nandan Vanam – the heaven's gardens. Parijata originated during the churning of the oceans, by the devas (deities) and asuras (demons).

Shachi, Indra's wife, adored the Parijata and wore the flowers in her hair each evening. She loved the adulation she received from all, wearing the flower, and as Indra's (the king of heaven) wife, she regarded this flower as her exclusive privilege, unshared with others.

Lord Krishna and his wife Satyabhama, once arrived at heaven. Indra had invited them in reciprocation for the help received from Lord Krishna. Indra requested them to stroll across the Nandan Vanam. The multicoloured splendour of the flowers there pleased Satyabhama immensely. Her gaze soon settled on the dainty Parijata flowers.

"I haven't seen such a flower before," remarked Satyabhama, "where did Indra get it from?"

Lord Krishna briefed her on its origin. He told her that Indra had carried it with him to the heavens, to plant it in Nandana Vanam.

Satyabhama thought over it and stated that Indra's action was unfair. Her feeling was that as many were involved in the ocean churning, Indra claiming exclusive rights to the Parijata tree was unjust. She requested Lord Krishna that she be allowed to carry it back to her garden at Dwarka, back on earth. She wanted to share the Parijata with all at Dwarka.

Lord Krishna smilingly consented. But, just as the Parijata tree was to be moved from heaven, carried on Garuda's back, guards at the heaven's gates stopped them. They indicated that it was Indra's property and taking it out from Nandana Vanam without his permission, amounted to stealing it – they would not permit that.

Satyabhama asked the guards to inform Indra that the plant would indeed go back to the earth and that if Indra thought it fit, he would have to fight Lord Krishna, to take back the plant. The guards carried this message to Indra.

Indra was livid with anger. He picked up the lightning, his chief weapon, to fight Lord Krishna. All devas and all the stars in heaven backed him in the fight.

Indra faced Lord Krishna with the might of his entire army while Lord Krishna stood alone, Garuda by his side. The ensuing battle, however, saw none surviving on Indra's side. Indra used his chief weapon, the lightning but against Lord Krishna, it was ineffective. Defeated and defenceless, Indra tried to run away, filled with remorse and shame.

Satyabhama laughed in amusement as she saw Indra trying to flee from there. She then called out to him and told him that he could keep the Parijata if he wanted. Satyabhama, as Indra's guest, was however not happy that Shachi had not even bothered to meet her or greet her at the heavens. That she thought was rude of her and upon learning that Shachi had selfishly held on to the Parijata plant, she was all the more keen to teach her a lesson.

Indra came over and sought Satyabhama's pardon. He admitted that it was very wrong of his wife to ignore his guest of honour. As retribution, he requested Satyabhama to carry the Parijata to the earth.

Thus, the Parijata flowers were brought to earth in a creative way, countering the ego of the *devas*.

A certain technique of creativity is called the '1 to 20 technique'. That is, whatever you want to create, generate 20 ideas. Then pick up one of the ideas that you feel is the most appropriate and generate 20 ways to bring that one idea it into reality. Then, choose the most appropriate one in that given situation and totally act to reach the desired result.

Reflection Point

Will you see a situation through special eyes to shed more light?

Are you courteous to others?

Have you been creative like getting the Parijata for the common good and yet teaching a lesson to the egoist?

Time Management

A German entrepreneur, in a recent International conference of CEOs at Hyderabad, asked me to narrate an Indian perspective of Time Management. All that I had to say was:

Parikshit, was the son of Abhimanyu and Uttara and also the grandson of Arjuna. He was the successor of Yudhisthira to the throne of Hastinapura. He was born only after the war ended.

Uttara was carrying their son in her womb when Abhimanyu was mercilessly and unfairly slain by the Kauravas. Later, Ashwathama attempted to kill the unborn child and its mother by directing the 'brahmastra' the most destructive weapon towards her tent, that was situated off the battlefield. She was saved by Lord Krishna, who was also the maternal uncle of Abhimanyu.

He was given the name Parikshit as he would search and test for the Supreme Lord, whom he had witnessed as an unborn child, across the world and within every human being.

Upon the commencement of the Kali-yuga, the dark age of sin, and the departure of Lord Krishna from the world, the five Pandava brothers retired. Young Parikshit was duly anointed as the king.

Once, Parikshit went hunting in the forest. Kali, the embodiment of Kali Yuga, appeared before him and sought permission from him, to enter his kingdom, which the king refused. Upon insisting, Parikshit allowed him four places to reside; where there is gambling, alcohol consumption, prostitution and gold. Kali smartly entered Parikshit's golden crown and corrupted his thoughts.

Parikshit strolled into sage Shringi's hut as he was thirsty. He found that the sage was in deep meditation. He bowed to him several times but as there was no response, he took a dead snake and threw it around the sage's neck. Later, when the sage's son heard of this incident, he cursed that the king would die of a snake bite within the next 7 days.

On hearing this, the king abdicated the throne for his son Janamejaya and spent his last 7 days listening to the discourses of Sage Sukadeva on Bhagavata. As prophesied, the snake king Takshaka bit Parikshit, and he left his mortal remains behind to attain salvation. He optimised the last 7 days of his life most dexterously.

What is interesting to note in Parikshit's life is – his vision to spend the last seven days of his life in the contemplation to attain the means to lead him to *moksha*, rather than frittering away time worrying about a curse. What takes many several births, he covered in a few days! This is time management even in a crisis as serious as one's own death!

As creatures bound to the material world, we are all ruled by time. Time appears to be a limited resource. If properly managed, it will enable you to stretch it, so as to accomplish more than what ad hoc approaches may. Time management in personal life is as scientific a discipline as (say), something like materials handling in the manufacturing industry. It is based on considerations of the available quantum, existing and anticipated demands, priority among competing demands etc. If you manage your time with professional precision, you will be able to divide your time among different tasks with demonstrable fairness and still be left with enough time to attend to your leisure and entertainment needs.

Identify What you Need to Accomplish

Sujatha has many commitments to fulfil as part of her work and personal life. At the beginning of the week, she is ready to contribute 100% of her energy, but as each day passes, her enthusiasm keeps flagging. As a result, she cannot fulfil her commitments. How can she solve her problem?

First, you must prioritise your commitments as per their importance to the overall objectives of your work. Suppose you must meet three clients on a given day, you cannot drop any of them from your list, yet, you can decide whom to meet first and whom last, among them. This is what is meant by prioritisation. This attitude will help you fight physical fatigue as well as the decline in enthusiasm.

Whatever choice you make in the prioritisation of your tasks, keep in mind that even this freedom to choose has its own bondage.

Now imagine I call you over to me and ask you to lift one of your legs. Perhaps you happen to lift your right leg. My instruction gave you two choices, but you decided to lift your right leg and not your left one. You were free to choose, but once you made a choice, you were bound to that because, once you lifted the right leg, you wouldn't be able to lift the other. One has to be at peace with one's decision. Similarly, our businesswoman is free to call on just one customer, increase the number to two, or decide to spend less time with the first two so that she can accommodate the third too. Hence, she should be at peace with her decision.

Remember that once you have made a choice, you have foreclosed other options. You cannot say that you would like to do this, that and the other. Our businesswoman can decide to meet all her important clients on the same day and end up feeling physically and mentally drained. Or she can choose differently and retain her stamina and enthusiasm.

Prioritise Your Priorities

◆ Look at your peak performance time and low-performance time.

◆ Do the most important thing in peak performance time and less important in low-performance time.

◆ Keep vigil and catch your time wasters.

◆ Learn to delegate.

◆ Thus plan accordingly your schedule giving yourself a healthy target.

◆ Understand how you are currently spending your time.

If you reflect a little and observe carefully, you will see that many who appear to be busy spend more time than required for a task. Most of you waste time without realising it.

How can you improve our awareness so that you are better organised and wasting less time and improve your scheduling?

Leisure Time is Important

Our businesswoman can also choose to take some leisure time. Don't think that leisure is a waste of time. It is, in fact, very important. You can come back after leisure, rejuvenated in spirit and produce better results. Taking some time off during busy days will keep you enthusiastic throughout the week. Leisure increases productivity, as any textbook in occupational psychology will tell you. Therefore, do not think that time spent on leisure is a waste. If you want to enjoy leisure and recreation, you should decide not to spend 100% of your time towards work.

You all work as if the number of hours at your disposal is infinite, but there are only 24 hours, each day. You must accommodate a lot within this limited time. If the time is limited, you must limit yourself some way or the other. Reduce the level of your personal commitment. Be prepared to delegate powers and responsibilities. It is not that you alone can take care of everything. You must learn to share work with competent assistants. Many refuse to delegate power as they feel that they are indispensable. Let others learn the ropes under your guidance.

What are the metaphysical dimensions of time? And how do you apply them in the corporate world?

If you closely observe each of your lifespans, it is spread over few years, say 82 years. If you further break down the years into days ... and days into hours... hours into minutes you arrive at a sum. The time ahead of you in minutes will give you a shocking reality. Therefore, to live for 82 years you should start to live in minutes. Every minute of your life adds and directs to 82 years. So totally live each minute in joy, spreading love and being creative.

Each minute hence lived well or otherwise determines the quality of your lives. If you can live the moment totally, time becomes the 'moment' of time.

If you want to live the quality life of Buddha or Lord Krishna in your lifetime of 82 years, live the moment 'now' as Lord Krishna or Buddha would have lived. The choice before you is to live 'here' and 'now' in totality.

Ways of Living

For most people, their present is a continuation of the past. Past hurts, upsets, incompleteness, resentment... flow into the present. Therefore, the past continues as the present. Their future is also a continuation of the present. What they are 'now' extends to the future if there is no transformation. Therefore, future is an extension of past passing through the present.

I have observed, however, that the convenience of external situation does not impact an individual if the transformation of time does not happen just as I have mentioned above.

In some, the complexities and turmoil that existed while in the role of a manager still exists even if they become MD. Hence Indian spiritual thought offers this unique possibility of time management of being in the 'present' and 'now'.

Let me present an interesting episode that I read recently.

Recently, when I was going to bed after using my bathroom, I started hearing the sound of drops of water from the tap in slow succession, but since it was dropping into an empty bucket, I decided to let it be.

But, alas! When I woke up the next morning, around 5 am, the bucket was almost full! I was surprised that just drops even in such slow succession could produce that much. I couldn't help it, 'Just drops?!' I questioned rhetorically.

But the following night, I made sure that the tap in my bathroom was closed completely and I checked the bucket and saw that it was empty, though wet. Then I went to sleep.

I guess you already know what I saw the next morning. The bucket was not wet as I had left it, but it was now dry!

Then I realised the importance of a drop and how much difference it can make in all contexts of one's life comparable to a dry tap.

Imagine letting the drops' dropping continuing for a year, I would be scooping with drums at the end of the year!

So, how about that drop of savings?

How about that drop of kindness and love every day?

How about a drop of reading useful books today and every day?

How about that drop of a verse of the scripture today and every day?

How about that drop of prayer today and every day?

How about a drop of worship today and every day?

How about a drop of steps towards your God-given dream today and every day?

How about a drop of giving into your heavenly account?

What virtue and discipline will you start today in little drops?

Never neglect the importance of a drop, for when the harvest time comes, you would have made a big difference.

Just drops make a difference!

Reflection Point

Can you be a light unto yourself?

Life is about how you frame your experience. The quality of your life is the quality of your inner communication, i.e., what you say to yourself. Transform Frustrations to Fascination!.

Communication Skills

A research fellow at a prestigious university sought a reply to this question – how do you unfold various aspects of communication – both internal to oneself and external to the world outside? Are there two sides that one has to manage and how?

Reflect on this parable.

A King with a defect in one eye and a leg asked all the painters in his kingdom to draw his portrait.

But no one was ready to draw, as it was difficult to show him as beautiful, with a defect in one eye and a leg.

One painter however agreed and drew a classic one.

It was such a fantastic painting that everyone was surprised.

He painted the King aiming for a deer in a hunt, targeting with one eye closed and a leg bent for it.

Why can't you all paint others like this – "softening their weaknesses and highlighting their strengths"?

You need to learn to soften others' weaknesses and bring their virtues to light.

Everyone asks you to communicate effectively, but what does that mean? The dictionary defines it as the exchange of information. Communication goes beyond mere data exchange through spoken words. It pertains to the intent behind the information and the emotions involved, providing a profound understanding of what the other person is really trying to say. You must be able to comprehend people without forcing your own opinions on anyone. At the same time, you should be able to stand up for yourself in difficult situations, without resorting to aggression and shouting. The words you speak are just the beginning; verbal communication makes up a small part of a much larger picture. A far larger part of it boils down to non-verbal cues that are given out and how much you listen to people. Added to this, are the cultural differences that communication must overcome. An Indian businesswoman may communicate very differently, in terms of gestures used, humour, eye contact etc. from an American man.

How does one navigate through such a layered and complex landscape, where there seems to be more exceptions than rules? As difficult as it seems, navigate you must, because the rewards far outweigh the efforts. Whatever the culture or the context, there are certain underlying principles that form the basis of effective communication.

Reflect on the modern day interpretation of the Bhagavad Gita in management that I recently heard.

An interesting conversation between Krishna and today's Arjuna.

Arjuna:- I can't find free time. Life has become hectic.

Krishna:- Activity gets you busy. But productivity sets you free.

Arjuna:- Why has life become complicated now?

Krishna :- Stop analysing life. It makes it complicated. Just live it.

Arjuna:- Why are we then constantly unhappy?

Krishna:- Worrying has become your habit. That's why you are not happy.

Arjuna:- Why do good people always suffer?

Krishna:- A diamond cannot be polished without friction. Gold cannot be purified without fire. Good people go through trials, but don't suffer.

With that experience, their life becomes better, not bitter.

Arjuna:- You mean to say such experience is useful?

Krishna:- Yes. In every term, Experience is a hard teacher. She gives the test first and the lessons later.

Arjuna:- Because of so many problems, we don't know where we are heading...

Krishna:- If you look outside you will not know where you are heading.

Look inside. Eyes provide sight. The heart provides the way.

Arjuna:- Does failure and hurt prevent you from moving in the right direction?

Krishna:- Success is a measure that's decided by others. Satisfaction is a measure decided by you.

Arjuna:- In tough times, how do you stay motivated?

Krishna:- Always look at how far you have come rather than how far you must go. Always count your blessing, not what you are missing.

Arjuna:- What surprises you about people?

Krishna:- When they suffer they ask, "Why me?" When they prosper, they never ask "Why me?"

Arjuna:- How can I get the best out of life?

Krishna:- Face your past without regret. Handle your present with confidence. Prepare for the future without fear.

Arjuna:- One last question. Sometimes I feel my prayers are not answered.

Krishna:- There are no unanswered prayers. Keep the faith and drop the fear. Life is a mystery to solve, not a problem to resolve. Trust me. Life is wonderful if you know how to live.

Listening

It is instinctive to begin the discussion by looking at how you speak, to express yourself. However, if you delve deeper into what it takes for effective communication, you will find that it begins with listening.

There is a saying in the Vedas, which means, first learn how to listen. Despite distractions, you should listen to what is being said, carefully. You should listen not only to the words but also learn to listen to the meaning, the feeling and the context. When you understand the significance of the context, you will capture something that cannot be conveyed by mere usage of words as vehicles. While you listen to a speaker or author, you should not waste time agreeing or disagreeing with the context. Your listening should be focused. Actual listening of this kind leads to a deeper cognition of reality. It will help you understand what your team members are really saying.

How can you learn to improve your listening skills to gain deeper cognition of reality?

Speaking

Managing a team or even an organisation will often require you to assert what needs to be done, in a firm yet polite way. Assertive, yet non-violent communication, is an essential tool in today's business world.

How to express negative incidents in a positive way and learn to say no?

One has to have a clarity that the incident is one dimension and the meaning we give it, is another dimension. Incidents are just happening and the interpretation you give to the incident so often colours the incident.

For example, you see a lion that attacks and kills a buffalo. Killing can be viewed as cruel but the act of the lion killing is part of survival for the lion. The brilliance is in the act of killing. If this killing is understood, there is another dimension that needs to be looked into. The incident is one thing, the meaning given to an incident is either uplifting or whipping. You have to manage to give uplifting meaning. In this lies the answer to the question.

Bhasmasura, a devotee of Lord Shiva performed a great penance to obtain a boon. Lord Shiva was pleased. Bhasmasura asked that he be granted the power that anyone whose head he touched with his hand should be reduced to ashes (bhasma).

Lord Shiva granted this request, but Bhasmasura there upon wanted to test the power of the boon and attempted to place his hand on the head of Lord Shiva. Lord Shiva moved away from the scene, and was chased by Bhasmasura.

Wherever Lord Shiva went, Bhasmasura chased him. Somehow, Lord Shiva managed to reach Lord Vishnu to seek a solution to this predicament. Lord Vishnu on hearing Lord Shiva's problem, agreed to help him out.

Lord Vishnu, in the form of Mohini, appeared in front of Bhasmasura. Mohini was so beautiful that Bhasmasura immediately fell in love with her. Bhasmasura asked her to marry him. She told him that she was very fond of dancing, and would marry him only if he could match her moves identically. Bhasmasura agreed to the match and hence they started dancing. The feat went for days on end.

As Bhasmasura matched the disguised Lord Vishnu's move by move, he began to let his guard down. While still dancing, Mohini, struck a pose where her hand was placed on top of her own head. As Bhasmasura imitated her, he was tricked into touching his own head, and hence Bhasmasura immediately turned into ashes, due to the power he had recently gained.

Sometimes, it is your internal soliloquy or the meaning you give, that burns you. Hence beware!

Body Language

Eye contact, the tone of voice, hand gestures and many other little things make up effective communication. They fall into the non-verbal channels of kinesics (eye contact, facial expressions and body language), haptics (touch) and proxemics (personal space) and can be interpreted in various ways, subject to cultural, societal and personal influences.

In Western cultures, for example, good eye contact is seen as a sign of honesty, whilst in certain Eastern cultures such as the Japanese one, prolonged eye contact is taken as a sign of rudeness. Your previous boss may have considered light body touches as uncomfortable but your current boss may use them to show friendliness. Use body language to convey positive feelings. Stand tall, smile, and maintain eye contact (provided the culture requires it). When you have an open and empathetic attitude, you create a space for clear and easy understanding where even difficult topics may be clearly expressed.

How can you learn to build trust and emanate well-meaning kindness during times of conflict? How do people moving in love attract other people towards them?

The absence of love is the presence of fear. When there is fear, it prevents the flow of love and generates more insecurity. This results in the absence of trust. The centre of love is trust while the centre of insecurity is fear.

You have to respect how you are operating. If it is out of fear or insecurity, then you can never be friend with the other. The fear generates its own justifying logic of not connecting to other person and thus you are overpowered by its justifying logic. You have to psychologically bathe yourself with prayer and understanding. Trust happens when your centre happens to be in love. So, look at others through the energy of love and that will give you the energy to deal with difficult situations.

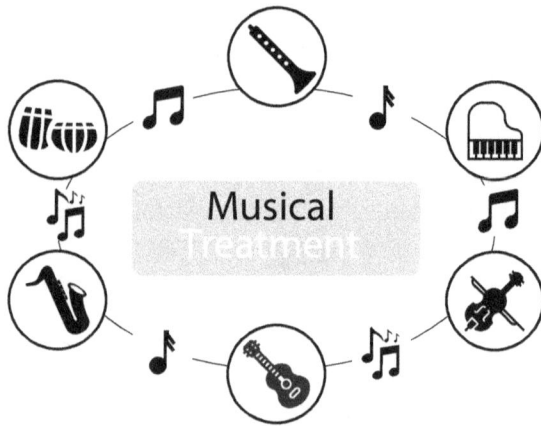

Musical Treatment

Every experience should have a musical treatment or emotional treatment and the experience of such treatment surfaces as assertiveness, compassion, detachment, love and happiness.

Use Humour

No matter what happens in life, keep in mind that all things are temporary. Even the most challenging conflict will pass with time. Using humour that is appropriate to a situation or circumstance can help dissolve resentment or frustration. It can even bring people in conflicting situations closer.

See commonality from a different point of view. Also, see the goodness in the other. Enhance your commitment to healing yourself and the other. In such a state, your state of being is bigger than the conflict.

Be Willing to Compromise – Agree to Disagree

You always don't have to agree with what someone is saying or doing, but if you value a person's point of view, you can agree to disagree. In that state of respectful understanding, compromise is possible. Such a compromise is healthy, for building a relationship.

Forgive and Forego

To forgive becomes easy when you understand that each one is fighting her own battle. Hence be compassionate. Also, understand no one can stir an empty cup. Further, when you don't hold hurt in a 'continuity mode', then you feel yourself healed. The fragrance of inner feeling is forgiveness and compassion.

There are different layers of communication which are to be deployed as a skill set in an individual. These are words, *lehar* (musical note or curve), a clear intention defined and communicated, and more importantly, any communication should add value to the receiver.

Reflection Point

Is there a half-truth situation... if so, which of the half side are you focused on?

Why Happiness Eludes us?

The successful owner of a fairly large enterprise, who had won many laurels, across all walks of life, both, personal and professional, wanted to know from me as to how to conquer the final frontier i.e., being happy always.

Why is happiness so elusive? Sage Patanjali tells us that it is due to the play of mind.

Your mind is not a substance. It is an activity complex. If you understand this, then you will know a lot. Take for example the activity of walking. We all know that walking is good. It has many benefits for health. But walking forever is harmful to the body. No one wants to walk endlessly, without reason, for that would be an abuse of walking. It is the same with the mind. Thoughts are useful; they are necessary. But when thinking is done and the purpose is achieved, the process should stop. Think when necessary; not when unnecessary. But are you able to do this?

No.

The solution Patanjali offers is - *chittavritthinirodaha or* cessation of the modification of the mind. This unnecessary activity of the mind has created chaos. A mind that creates chaos should be ended. This ending is called *chittavritthinirodaha.*

Why is the mind always flitting here and there? The restless mind is not able to discover *ananda* or the joy of existence. The mind likes to live in lies. The mind does not wish to live in truth.

This is a very grave and sad reality.

And what is one of the greatest lies of the mind? That 'in the future, I will be happy.'

Here we see another problem: we either want happiness in our *samsara* (cycle of death and rebirth to which life in the material world is bound) or we want *nirvana* (a state of being unbound to the world), but the wanting never ceases. This wanting puts us in the future. We think the future will be our saviour. Why do we think this way? This is because we have not seen the richness of the present. This is the problem.

Therefore, the mind needs the lie that the future is going to be 'my saviour.' A future canvas is thereby necessary for the mind to project its dreams and expectations. Hence, the projecting mind, that looks to the future, is never at ease.

Such a mind is noisy. Noisy and unable to enjoy the present moment, it cannot digest any experience to its fullest. These undigested experiences, then, are at the root of unhappiness and sorrow.

Very often patterns and emotions of the mind influence perceptions and that guides the relationships with others.

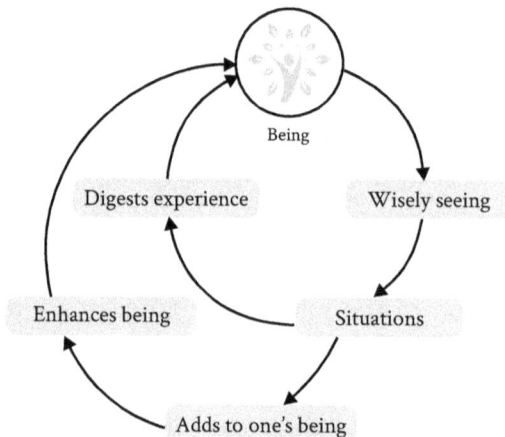

If one searches through intelligence and if that becomes an operating system, there would be wisdom in action.

Reflect on Shakuni's life, in the Mahabharata.

Shakuni was deeply hurt by the fact that his sister Gandhari was married to the blind king Dritharashtra. He left Gandhar and lived with his sister in Hastinapur with the hidden agenda to destroy the kingdom for the injustice meted out to his sister.

He loved Duryodhana but his hidden agenda over-rode everything else, when guiding him to the wrong direction. This was instrumental in causing the epic war. He was oblivious of the ways his hidden agenda played out and that took over him. Thus, his love for both Gandhari and Duryodhana lacked purity.

Was it Shakuni's designs or his intelligence, that weighed higher in operation?

His designs or plans, destroyed him and others too. Self-introspect on a scale of 1:10 and cleanse yourself.

Reflect on Ravana's life in the Ramayana.

If we study the life of Ravana, we find that he was the lord of three worlds, had immense wealth, had mastery of the Vedas, was Lord Shiva's ardent devotee and wedded to the most beautiful woman as queen... yet he never rejoiced life as a present. His mind was restless and greedy.

He was engaged in unwanted pursuits and that brought about his annihilation.

Reflect on this episode that I recently read in a flight.

There was a Jewish man who had a bakery, in a town, in Germany. He always said, "You know why I'm alive today?"

He said, "I was a kid, just a teenager at the time in Germany, when the Nazis were mercilessly killing Jews.

We were on the train being taken to Auschwitz by the Nazis. Night came and it was deathly cold in that compartment.

The Germans left us on the side of the tracks overnight, sometimes for days, without any food. There were no blankets to keep us warm. Snow was falling everywhere. Cold winds were hitting our cheeks, every second. We were hundreds of people on that terribly cold night. No food. No water. No shelter. No blankets.

The blood in our bodies started freezing. It was becoming ice.

Beside me, there was a beloved elderly Jewish man from my hometown. He was shivering from head to toe and looked terrible. So I wrapped my arms around him to warm him up.

I hugged him tightly to give him some heat. I rubbed his arms, his legs, his face, his neck. I begged him to try to be alive.

I encouraged him.

All night long, I kept this man warm this way.

I was tired and freezing in the cold. My fingers were numb, but I didn't stop rubbing heat into that old man's body.

Hours and hours went by. Finally, morning came and the sun began to shine. I looked around to see the other people...

To my horror, all I could see were frozen bodies. All I could hear was deathly silence!

Nobody else in that cabin was alive. That freezing night killed them all.

They died from the cold. Only two people survived: the old man and I.

The old man survived because I kept him warm... and I survived because I was warming him.

May I tell you the secret to survival in this world where we all have trouble and needs?

When you warm other people's hearts, you will remain warm yourself!

When you support, encourage and inspire others, then you will discover support, encouragement and inspiration in your own life as well."

That's the secret to happiness.

Reflection point

Is this message fully internalised, imbibed and assimilated?

Are you giving warmth to others and to yourself... in the process of giving warmth, are you receiving warmth?

Can you see the inter-play of the unconscious hidden agendas in your life? Identifying the inner cobwebs and clearing them is a great service. Are you practising this in your life daily? Please audit yourself.

Mind Management

In a conference recently, one of the HR directors asked, "Among all forms of management, the mind management appears to be most complicated. How does one address this issue? This is affecting my life."

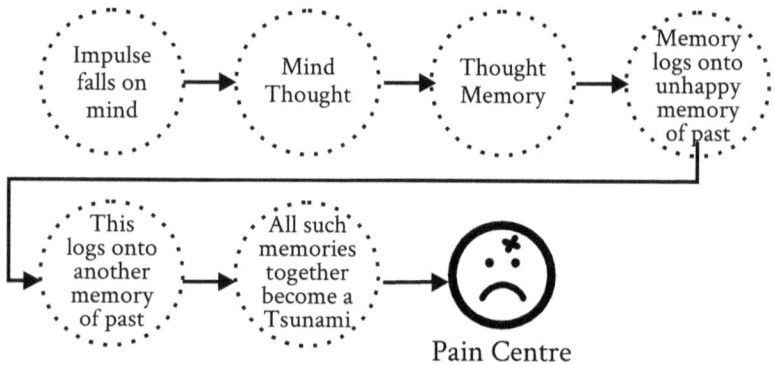

Impulse falls on mind → Mind Thought → Thought Memory → Memory logs onto unhappy memory of past → This logs onto another memory of past → All such memories together become a Tsunami. → Pain Centre

You need a mind but beware of the type of mind. It can give you sorrow and also, the absence of sorrow. So what type of mind should you have? Patanjali goes on to say: your thoughts are of five modifications. What are these five modifications of the mind?

They are: *pramana, viparyaya, vikalpa, nidra* and *smriti*.

Pramana refers to the right knowing. What does thought do? It always compares to something else. Thought compares, and in that comparison, you feel incomplete. When thought compares, you become incomplete. But if you can bring in awareness, a thought that doesn't compare, but appreciates and focuses on the moment, then you will see the fullness of the moment. This is the right knowing. *Pramana* also includes logical and experiential proof and the means of right perception. Can you bring thought without unnecessary comparison? This is the real austerity.

Viparyaya pertains to wrong knowing. Thought guided by memory is merely a representation of the past. It is an experience; a representation of an experience, not an experience *per se*. In the absence of experience, the richness of the moment is lost. When the richness of the moment is absent, you experience sorrow. Sorrow creates psychological grooves in the mind. The mind revels in such grooves.

Thought also comes from likes and dislikes: 'I like this', 'I don't like that'. Who do these likes and dislikes serve? They serve the ego. When thought guided by generals that are 'like' and 'dislike' serve the king, the ego, then you experience the distorted perception.

So, can there be a knowing without being propelled by likes and dislikes or being guided by the ego? If such a thought is possible, then you have the right awareness.

Vikalpa is imagination or mental construct. Every thought conjures so many images. You have an image of yourself. Thought has an image. When I have an image of myself and of you, then I don't really connect to you, and you don't really connect to me because the image gets in the way and plays a strong role. Observe how thought creates an image, expectation and conclusion. Therefore, I see you and you see me through this image, we are seeing each other through expectations and conclusions projected by thought.

Nidra means the ability to still thought. If you can do this consciously, this is called *samadhi*. Nature gives you this experience, like a trailer for a movie, through sleep.

Smriti stands for memory and recollection.

Memory can be empowering or victimising. The unintelligent use of memory constantly recollects the victimisation of what has happened and relives it. This keeps you in the non-resourceful state.

Intelligently managing all the above five modifications of thought is to bring forth resourceful state in an individual.

The play of five different modifications of thought can be summed up from the life of Karna from Mahabharata.

Karna, the uncrowned hero, was one of the most captivating characters of Mahabharata. A legend, not only was he known for his unmatched skills but also for his generosity and integrity. A great warrior, he was often considered as the "anti-hero" due to his loyalty to Duryodhana, the leader of the wrong side.

He was resentful as he did not know his biological parents. His foster parents – Radha and Athiratha, supported him with utmost love. He always recalled fondly, as to how much his mother loved him. "She's the only one who loved me for who I am," he said.

Competence and destiny's will made him Angaraja – the king of state of Anga. He was also a big king's confidante. Duryodhana considered him as dear and heeded to his advice. He had everything that life could offer. It should have made him happy that though being a charioteer's son, he became a king.

He did not give up his resentment. He could not come to terms with the fact that he was being labelled as suta or "low-born". Throughout life, he complained about this. At all times, he nourished bitterness within himself about his so-called low birth.

This bitterness turned a wonderful human being into a very nasty character in the Mahabharata. He was a great human being and showed his greatness in many situations. But because of his bitterness, everything turned wrong in his life.

What Shakuni said or did, did not matter to Duryodhana as much as Karna's advice did. It was Karna's word that always sealed the deal. After everything was decided, he would look at Karna, "What shall we do?" Karna could have very easily turned the direction of the whole story.

His life alternated through patches of tragedy and sacrifice. He displayed a sense of sacrifice continuously. No good, however, came of it as he was devastated by the one thing that mattered the most – he wanted to be somebody that he was not; at least so, was the society's view. He continuously blundered due to this obsession.

He was an intelligent man. He had enough sense to see that Duryodhana was doing the wrong things. But he wasn't a passive participant. He actively supported Duryodhana's actions. If only Karna had used his intelligence rather than loyalty and gratitude, Duryodhana's life could have been saved. Resultantly, he committed blunder after blunder.

When Lord Krishna came as an emissary of the Pandavas for peace, he spoke to Karna. Lord Krishna said, "Why are you doing this to yourself? This is not what you are. Let me tell you what your parentage is. Kunti is your mother and your father is Surya."

Karna broke down. He always wanted to know who he was and where he came from. He always longed to know who was it that had let him off in the river in a little box. Suddenly, he realised that he had been actively trying to nurture hatred towards the five Pandavas, even though they were his brothers. His loyalty to Duryodhana, however, made him believe that he had to hate these five people. Though there was no hatred in his heart, he had worked it up all the time and had come out meaner than anyone.

If Shakuni said something, he would supplement that. And he wouldn't stop there because he was always working up his hatred trying to prove his loyalty, for all that Duryodhana had done for him. He was a wonderful person but he continuously made mistakes. All your lives are like that – if you make one wrong choice, you may take ten years or more to recover, won't you? Karna never recovered because he took too many wrong turns.

Lord Krishna asked Karna to abandon Duryodhana and join his brothers (the Pandavas). Lord Krishna offered the entire kingdom to him.

Karna, however, did not want to desert his friend Duryodhana, who had stood by him at critical junctures in life. Karna knew that his side was going to lose. Karna even knew that it was the God himself (Lord Krishna) was making him that offer! He, however, valued his friendship and loyalty higher.

His was again, a classic case of not rejoicing the talent bestowed upon him by existence. He was not sourcing his energy from his inborn talents, but sourcing it from the victimisation of injustice done to him.

Did he intelligently manage the five different modifications of thought?

Reflection Point

How often is there a prayerful pause, prayerful shock and prayerful direction that you give to yourself?

Check your life – is it complex like Karna or simple like Vidura?

Transform Frustrations to Fascination!

Stopping a Chattering Mind

Swamiji, I appreciate that we should manage our mind and that's a task in itself. But, it appears that the mind is constantly in a web of thoughts, on which we seldom have control. How do we deal with a chattering mind? A PhD student wanted me to answer.

I told him to reflect on this episode.

A Zen Master was on his customary stroll in serene surroundings. A student requested the Master as to whether he could walk with him, just to draw on the energy from his presence. The Master turned him down as the student was too talkative. The young man, however, promised to keep silent throughout the walk. They moved together in perfect silence, throughout the night and reached the top of a hill by sunrise. There, they were greeted by the brilliance of the sun, as dawn broke out.

"Beautiful," the student uttered.

The Master turned to him in disgust and said, "You will never walk with me again. You are too talkative."

In Zen, one need not resort to language either for thought or for communication. You eat something and say, 'beautiful'. You are telling yourself that the food is good, but the moment you use the word *beautiful*, you are putting your thought about the food into a particular category. That one word takes over your world of experience. The association between the word and the experience starts governing your later thoughts and perceptions, your likes and dislikes in food as well as other areas too. When you eat food, some other time, this impression carries itself over your experience and you judge the food as good or bad on that basis.

> No experience of food can ever be fresh: each new experience is compared to your previous experiences. We are in a prison house of our previous judgements.

This results from your tendency to verbalise even your intimate thoughts, nay your inability to think, other than in linguistic terms, in words and sentences. When I say you must meditate in silence, what I mean is that you should try to liberate your thought form the domination of language.

Reflect on this.

Our minds are like monkeys. When monkeys get wounded, they won't let the wounds be. Instead, they keep scratching, turning the wounds septic. If only they'd leave their wounds alone, they'd heal naturally.

Most of your minds are like these monkeys: you keep harping on some issues which then fester and infect your whole being. So, you should learn to stop your chattering mind and allow silence to teach you many things.

This ability cannot be acquired overnight: it comes from practice. You will ask me how you can ever get to the stage of pure thought.

> "
> How can anyone think independently of language? Consider yourself not as an active participant, but as a witness to what is happening. Distance yourself. "

Can you observe the functioning of your mind? Incidences do happen around you constantly. What type of a mind do you possess, to deal with such instances?

Yet again, drawing inspiration from the Mahabharata, you find that Duryodhana's inability to stop his chattering mind, was one of his biggest weaknesses. That apart, a big, and that too, a king-sized ego, was the root cause of the bloody war.

Rahul had been constantly disturbed by the many developments around him that did not meet his expectations. He felt that he was being constantly kicked around, like a football, through these incidents. Hence his work had become a movement of suffering. How could he work in such a workspace?

What is that he has to specially take care in his work area?

The following examples when reflected should give a way out to Rahul.

The human mind is like a television set with 1000 channels. If you turn on Buddha, you see Buddha. If you turn on sorrow, you see sorrow. Do not let any single channel dominate you.

Experience is one thing. Framing of an experience is another thing altogether for many.

I would like to share a narration someone shared it with me.

A young woman was sitting at her dining table, worried about the taxes to be paid, housework to be done and to top it all, her family was coming over for Thanksgiving the next day. She was not feeling very thankful at that time.

As she turned her gaze sideways, she noticed her young daughter scribbling furiously in her notebook.

"My teacher asked us to write a paragraph on 'Negative Thanksgiving' for homework today," said the daughter.

"She asked us to write down things that we are thankful for, things that make us feel not so good in the beginning, but turn out to be good after all."

With curiosity, the mother peeked into the book. This is what her daughter had written:

"I'm thankful for the final exams because that means school is almost over.

I'm thankful for bad-tasting medicine because it helps me feel better.

I'm thankful for waking up to the alarm clock because it means I'm still alive."

It then dawned upon the mother, that she had a lot of things to be thankful for!

She thought again...

She had to pay taxes, but, that meant she was fortunate to be employed. She had housework to do, but, that meant she had her own home to live in.

She had to cook for her family for Thanksgiving, but, that meant she had a family with whom she could celebrate.

We generally complain about the negative things in life, but, we fail to look at its positive side. What's the positive in your negatives?

Look at the better side of life, this day, and make your day a great one.

Reflection Point

Will you see situations around you with special eyes, to draw inspiration?

Managing Stress

After one of my sessions, I was watching a serene sunset, in a reflective mood, from the balcony of my hotel room, recently in Goa. One of the participants, a senior top management functionary of an Indian multi-national company, knocked at the door and somehow pleaded that I spend time on his burning issue – stress at work paralysing him almost and ways to deal with it. He said it was getting impossible to manage stress and many unfair incidents that had happened in his life only added to his being more stressful. How could he handle them?

I wondered where to begin from. Pausing for a while, I continued,

One of the classical ways of managing stress, is to be inspired by the way Kunti, in the Mahabharata, handled her life.

Her life can be summed up as under:
- Got separated from her real parents.
- Had to give up her first son, whom she set adrift in the river.
- Had to live with her husband in the forest despite being the queen.
- Lived as a celibate most of her life though she had a husband.
- Lost her husband in youth.
- Had to live with those who conspired against her children.
- Helplessly watched as her sons were conspired against, and attempts were made to kill them.
- Moved into the forest along with her children to escape from the fire.
- Helplessly saw her daughter-in-law being misbehaved with.
- Got separated from her children when they went to the forest again.
- Saw her son kill another son.
- Saw all her grandsons killed.

Yet we can learn a great lesson from her of creating the great heroes of Mahabharata where she guided them to uphold *dharma* and thus making great leaders out of them.

Do you lay awake at night worried by the events of the day? Does the uncertain future make you apprehensive? In today's corporate world, stress appears to be synonymous with management. High-pressure deadlines, demanding clients, reaching for nearly impossible targets – it may seem like juggling a million balls in the air. How can we handle it better? Worrying will never help.

Worry is like a rocking chair. It keeps you busy but leads you nowhere. So, if there are high targets, feel passionate about them. Bring in the emotion of enthusiasm and passion and then your corporate goals will inspire you. Keep in mind that emotion is energy in motion. Learn to bring the best emotion and that will relieve you of your stress. Learn to be a part of a solution rather than be a victim of the problem. Here are a few suggestions, as to how to do it.

Don't Fear the Result

At the root of it, stress occurs when you feel you are in a hurry and there is anxiety over the end results from what you might be doing. It is an indication that you are fighting with something, rather than learning to use challenges creatively to teach you lessons. For example, if you cannot sleep, instead of grappling with it, (say) by forcing yourself to sleep or internally complaining and feeling miserable, use that energy - take a walk; do some exercise. Whenever you are under stress, don't be miserable, don't get angry or anxious, but welcome it. That energy would prepare you to accept it. Such an action is born out of fullness.

Buddha has beautifully said that we don't experience whatever 'is'. We must learn to experience whatever is, simply as it is. Very few of us can do this because the 'experiencer' pollutes the experience.

> In fact, if you have lived your stress wisely and creatively, then relaxation will happen automatically. The art of wise living is in the ability to use whatever that life gives you, rather than being miserable from what you want from life.

Manage Your Thoughts

Look at stress in another way. Let us say a situation is giving you stress. Is it really the situation that is causing you difficulties? Learn to question it. When you question:–

◆ You will find that it is not the situation, but your interpretation of it that causes stress.

◆ Any given situation will perhaps create 10% of the stress. The remaining 90% is psychological.

◆ It is caused by the fear of what may happen.

◆ Note that fear is a movement of thought.

◆ The impact of thought is usually far greater on a person than the mere impact of a situation.

For example, when your boss shouts at you, you get hurt and, that hurt creates stress. The words of your boss are just words, aren't they? How can words hurt? The word 'idiot' is merely a word, and so the word 'idiot' cannot hurt. What hurts is the meaning you give it, and how you interpret the word. That interpretation is yours. Don't interpret it in a hurting way. That way you will not be hurt. Hurt or upset, whether you justify it or not, is self-damaging. So, refuse to get hurt and that decision will give you more power.

Learn to Respond – not React

An important lesson that the ancient Indian scriptures teach us is that whatever may be the *paristiti* or situation in life, learn to respond and not react.

Responding is called *anukriya*. Reacting is called *pratikriya*.

The more you react, the more your quality of consciousness becomes hellish. So long as your consciousness is merely rooted in reaction, you can never be a 'giver'. You need to be a 'giver' if you are going to be successful in the corporate sector. We all must give our time, energy and effort to make a business or career successful. If our energy is being used up in reactions, rather than appropriate responses, then our time and effort are consumed in negative thoughts that can destroy what we have built.

Recognise the Good – Calm Down

There is a sickness in living that every one of us falls prey to – we don't realise what we have. Our job is good in its own way. It provides us with a means to support ourselves and our families. Let us recognise and validate it. Our body is good. It works every day to give us the energy to do what we like. We don't validate this anymore.

Remember to take moments in your hectic schedule to recognise and validate the good that you have.

Simple meditation techniques for stress relief can be:

Take a deep breath and while exhaling chant 'Om' (Om is a composite of A, U, and M)

While chanting, focus on the sound U in 'Om'. By doing so, the mind is stilled and focused.

While chanting, observe navel centre is pulled in. This is a mystic centre. This is a source of connection with one's mother and hence mystic.

So, inhale and exhale with 'Om'. Feel the vibration of U in 'Om'. Feel the navel centre being pulled in while chanting. This has to be repeated for at least ten minutes in one sitting.

In the process, discover a mysterious spiritual centre in you. For more details on the significance and benefits of chanting 'Om', refer subsequent chapter on Om.

Relax — be Joyous and Laugh

A politician sees youngsters leaving everything behind to go and join an ashram. He asks one young man, "Why are you going to that guru?"

The youngster replies, "Because when I look at my guru, I feel that God exists."

The politician asks, "What do you feel when you see me?"

"That God can make mistakes."

Sometimes you act as if smiling is like paying taxes to the Government. There is no emotion in people, anymore. Feel your targets, feel the joy of your work and automatically, stress reduces. The moment you have the power of feeling your emotions, feeling your joy, you will be bigger than money, bigger than success and bigger than failure. All too often, people focus on improving their minds, but not their hearts.

Bringing joy to Your Life

There is an interesting tale from Mahabharata about the conversation that takes place between Karna and Vidura.

Karna at some time in his life narrated to Vidura how he was brought up by a charioteer and was called as sutaputra (son of a charioteer), a tag that he had to live with for his life. Further, he was insulted on many occasions citing his lowly birth status in those days.

Vidura cited a remarkable analogy from his own life that was worthy of a man of wisdom. He stated that though he himself was a dasiputra or son of a servant, he never whipped himself for his birth. Further, he added that he was accepted as the Prime Minister of Hastinapur for his ability and greatly respected.

In a macro sense, Karna did nothing extraordinarily wrong in his life, he couldn't be blamed solely for any mishap that occurred, but still, he is considered to be a grey-shaded character in the Mahabharata.

The circumstances being similar with respect to birth... here is a great warrior, always known as a giver, silently whipping himself for the unfairness meted to him by the society. On the other hand, Vidura was more prudent in accomplishing excellence and reached a worthy status, not affected by his birth status.

Reflection Point

Can you be a light unto yourself and dispel inner darkness?

How are you framing your experience of injustice, faced by you, in your life?

Managing Relationships

A young man working with a conglomerate of a well-known financial brand meets me. He is dejected, shattered, agitated within himself and, with tears rolling out confesses, "Swamiji, I am at the crossroads. All my relationships have touched the lowest rung... to such an extent that I am totally at a loss as to figure out where to begin from."

Reflect on this.

Lord Krishna was Arjuna's true friend, guide and philosopher. Though Arjuna was the best archer and the most favoured pupil of Dronacharya, in times of crisis, it was Lord Krishna who supported him. Arjuna was married to Krishna's sister, Subhadra, whose grandson was saved, in time, to be the torch bearer for the next generation after the Mahabharata war. Even during Draupadi's court mishap of disrobing after Yudhistira's loss in the dice game, it was Lord Krishna who came to the rescue and prompted Arjuna to acquire divine weapons for the ensuing Mahabharata war.

When Arjuna was deeply deluded and refused to fight the war, it was Lord Krishna who dispelled his lingering doubts. Arjuna's attachment and dilemma came to fore as he stood up to fight his relatives in the Kaurava camp that consisted his cousins, grandfather and his guru. Some of his most revered and loved ones, were standing in opposition, with a mighty army, to fight the Pandavas. It is at this crucial juncture that Lord Krishna gave the message of Bhagavad Gita to Arjuna. Arjuna saw a true inspirational guru in Lord Krishna. He was instructed by Lord Krishna to perform his duty and take on the challenges facing him, to restore Dharma. It is indeed a reflection of a true relationship which has few parallels, in any saga.

Arjuna was an instrument which Lord Krishna used, to sing the divine song – Bhagavad Gita for the benefit of mankind, across generations.

Look at this diagram carefully and employ the technique.

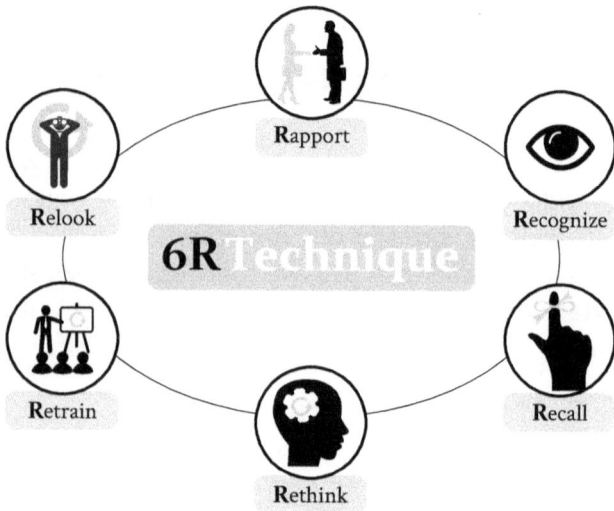

As the saying goes, no man is an island. Human beings are social creatures and relationships play a large role in defining the quality of your life. This is especially true in management, where human resources form the most important assets of any company.

Effective managers know that to bring about the best output, human connections must be cultivated and nurtured. A significant part of that nurturing process involves understanding what the core qualities of good relationships are. Once these are identified, it is then a question of how to cultivate them in your day-to-day interactions.

Disagreement is part and parcel of any relationship. One must be reconciled to this fact of life.

Creatively converting disagreement into productivity is a challenge.

> " The core of mutual respect is in accepting the potential of each other and to operate from the belief that the relationship would grow into a beautiful force in due course of time. "

It is something like the seed becoming a tree. Look at the lives of many great people. They were very ordinary to start with, but when their potential expanded, they become a force to reckon with. Steve Jobs, Mahatma Gandhi and many others are few examples that you can recall and ponder over.

Mythology tells how Prahlada though born as an *asura* (demon) became one of the greatest devotees of the Lord.

Trust

When he first started working, Arvind was willing to trust people and take them at their word. Very soon, he was betrayed by the very colleague whom he considered a friend. Unfortunately, he still must work with that colleague regularly and this affects their work relationship. Since then, he has struggled to trust people, because it is difficult to gauge a person's sincerity and safer to guard against the belief that everyone will cheat him.

Is it naive to trust people? How can you trust and also guard against the ill-will of others?

Trust is at the core of every relationship. How can you learn to trust others?

How do you overcome hurt and trauma when your trust has been betrayed, so that you can still manage to work effectively when you are compelled to work with the very people that you feel have betrayed you?

Firstly, Arvind has to learn not to be trapped by betrayal. Since he is trapped by betrayal, that trapped and bound energy interjects into others; so does his struggle with trust too.

If you can look at betrayal or hurt and approach it from freedom, that freedom would free you from the incident, however bad that experience may be.

When freedom is the foundation to which you relate, it has intelligence. That intelligence, will trust and doubt, as may be needed. Such trust and doubt results from freedom and hence, it is not a limitation, else, it would be foolish to trust a thief or criminal, but would definitely be wise to doubt a thief or criminal.

Steps to Establish Trust

Trust is the core of a relationship only when it emerges from intelligence. Learn to trust your intelligence.

How to overcome hurt is to understand that each one is fighting one's own battle and each one is entangled in one's own psychological pattern and disorder. Thus, to be compassionate with them through a deep sense of understanding and, commitment to empower them, is the core of effective relationship.

Mutual Respect and Welcoming of Diversity

In any work environment, there will be many people and ideas. Invariably, situations will arise when you disagree with your team members and colleagues.

What is at the core of mutual respect that can overcome these barriers of disagreement? Reflect deeper on it.

Mindfulness

Mindfulness in the Buddhist paradigm: being constantly aware of and taking responsibility for actions and words that can impact the people around you.

Open Communication

What it means to communicate openly and honestly when the truth is sometime a tricky thing to deal with.

Building Good Relationships

The key to relationship building is active listening.

How do you cultivate good listening skills?
- Firstly be positive and genuinely appreciate others.
- People naturally gravitate towards those with a positive mindset and understanding.

What is the secret to keeping a positive attitude on a day-to-day basis?

Avoid Gossiping

Savita learnt through the grapevine that her colleagues have been making some character maligning statements about her because of her lifestyle choices. Though she never indulges in such gossip herself, she's having a hard time dealing with things that are being said about her. It is beginning to affect her, both, personally as well as professionally and she doesn't know how to handle this challenge.

Why do you feel the need to gossip? How do you avoid it? How do you manage the topic of negative statements being said?

Identify your relationship needs and manage your boundaries.

Every relationship you know will have different needs. You will also have different expectations from every relationship. How to set expectations to match your needs is a key to maintaining good relationships.

Work on a relationship Matrix: how it can help you set boundaries and expectations in your relationships and how it can nurture those relationships effectively.

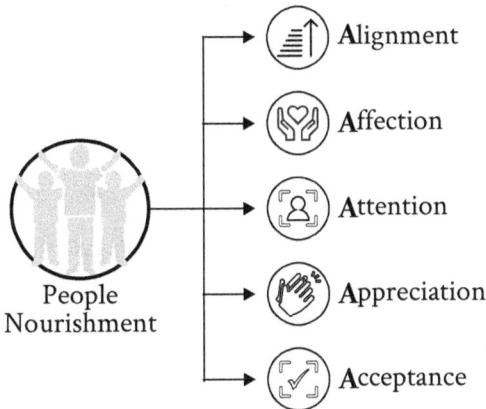

People Nourishment → Alignment, Affection, Attention, Appreciation, Acceptance

Managing Difficult Relationships

Praveen has a boss whom he just doesn't like. He finds it impossible to deal with him regularly, but he has no other

way out than quitting his job, something he doesn't want to do. He doesn't know how to deal with this situation.

What lies in the nature of dislike? Why is it that there are some people that you just do not like?

How can you overcome dislike and manage people that you find as difficult?

How do you build a good relationship or even manage a working relationship with someone you just don't like?

Reflect on this example that someone shared with me for a possible answer.

Flowers are beautiful and adorable. Across ages, they have been used on certain occasions. They have brought joy to celebrations like birthdays, weddings, anniversaries and in times of happiness. They are synonymous with the feeling of love. On the other hand, they have also been used on sad occasions like death.

Flowers are God's gift to mankind. Their colours and fragrances can brighten any day. They can linger in our thoughts for a long time.

Apart from the beauty, fragrance and cheer that they bring, they also teach us an important lesson in life.

The rose and the lotus are two beautiful flowers. A rose has thorns. Yet the rose does display its beauty and spread its fragrance. The lotus is born in muddy, murky waters. In such dirt, the lotus continues to bloom and show its beauty.

We all reflect similar attributes too. Everyone has something positive or the other, which is like the beauty of the rose or the lotus. At the same time, there are negative traits too, like the rose's thorns or the murky water around a lotus.

What you choose to display is important. Like thorns, you may have hindrances and obstacles. Like muddy waters, you may not have a good past. You have the choice as to what you want to become.

You can choose to highlight the thorns or the muddy waters. You can also choose to bloom like the rose or the lotus. It all depends on the choice that you make. Life is not about fate. It is about choice.

God has blessed you with free will. It's a gift that has been given to no one else but mankind. This free will allows you to make a choice instead of giving into fate.

You can use your free will to lose yourself to circumstances or stand up to display the beauty in you.

Good or bad... the choice is always yours.

Reflection Point

Will you employ your spiritual key when faced with a situation like this?

Have you explored connecting with others through 'mind' and 'heart' keeping your 'being' open?

Are you Looking Within?

Recently, I got a beautiful gift. One of my new students told me, "My biggest tension points, Swamiji, are my husband and you. My husband is a tension point, and you are another tension point."

Why did she say this?

अन्धगजन्यायः

The maxim of the blind men and the elephant.

Three visually challenged people approached a tame and docile elephant, to get an idea of the animal. One felt its trunk, another its legs, the third, its tail. The first man, who had felt the trunk, described it as a fat serpent. The second man, who had felt its legs, described it as four pillars. The third one who had passed his hands on the tail, described it as a piece of stout rope, tapering gradually with loose fibres at the end. They began to fight amongst themselves, with each clinging to his description as being the right one.

This maxim is used in cases where an imperfect, partial or one-sided view of anything is taken.

Let me answer this question by recounting the famed story of the churning of the ocean of milk. It is said that the *devas* (gods) and *asuras* (demons) decided to work together to churn the ocean of milk to get precious *amrutha* (nectar). However, before they derived the *amrutha,* there was *visha* (poison). So potent was the poison that it threatened to destroy all.

Reflect on this story in a contemporary context allowing for some flexibility in thought.

The great Lord Shiva decided to swallow this poison to save others from its toxicity. He could keep it in his neck, which turned blue as a result, hence earning him the name of Neelakanta. With his whole body burning with the poison, Lord Shiva headed to the Himalayas to cool himself. He failed. Then he tried to get the river Ganga from heaven to flow onto his head, and that did not help either. Nothing that Lord Shiva tried could cool his body; so potent was the poison.

Then Lord Shiva did the Ramanamajapa. This eventually cooled Lord Shiva. It was then that Lord Shiva told his wife Parvathi, the story of Ramayana, the epic tale of Lord Rama to reflect deeper meaning.

What can you learn from this? Those external or material objects cannot cool you. It was only spiritual awakening from the *Ramanamajapa,* that did help Lord Shiva cool down. Unless there is a spiritual awakening, you cannot cool yourselves.

What happens when you go on looking outside of yourself? At some point, the outside reality does not match with your inner expectations. And this leads to reactions. When you get reactions, you heat up, just as Lord Shiva's body did. Where do you go with that heated body? Some of you go to Kailash, and yet others to a bar. Whenever you react to the heat, you say, 'Oh I am reacting because of my husband; I am reacting because of my wife' etc. You create tension points.

My new student explained why I was her tension point.

"You always tell me, I am responsible for my tension. How can I be responsible for my tension? My husband is an idiot. He is responsible for my tension. And you are supporting my husband by saying I am responsible for the tension. So, my big tension is you Swamiji!" she said.

You have a picture of somebody – the image of someone. When dealing with someone, if their picture does not match your expectation, there is tension.

But the intelligent question that you need to ask yourself is - should the map fit the territory or territory fit the map?

Look at the life of Duryodhana and Dhritarashtra, in the Mahabharata.

Duryodhana always had set his eyes on the throne. Though his father was the king, his anger swelled and within himself, he continued to burn out of hate and jealousy, towards the Pandavas.

Hatred and anger were his constant companions and stirred negative thoughts in him throughout his life. Though his father had a throne, yet he continued to despair. Thus, his whole life was wasted in getting the elusive throne.

This is a case history of an ideal situation that did not match the reality.

Now let me ask again, why did she say this? It was because I did not meet her expectations to say that her husband was responsible for her tensions. I had to tell this lady that I was not responsible for her tension. These reactions occurred within her, because she was not delving within. She was outward looking.

So, I ask you again, are you looking within?

Reflection Point

Will you see situations around through special eyes to shed more light?

Are you coming from the 'blaming pattern' or the 'learning pattern'?

Aim big and Achieve big

A businessman's son, an upcoming entrepreneur, is constantly battered by his peers, parents and relatives on how he has not set his goals higher when compared with his friends who we are doing well. Says he, "Swamiji, do you have any mantra for achieving big things in life"?

I opened my interaction with an incident narrated below.

There was once a very philanthropic man who wanted to honour the most courageous person in town. He said he would give a large sum of money to anyone who accomplished a certain feat. All the people of the town gathered to know what that feat was. The philanthropist explained that whosoever could swim from one end of the swimming pool to the other, in the town, would get a large sum of money.

This seemed to be without any challenge until the philanthropist added: "But, bear in mind, there are 20 odd crocodiles in the pool."

When this 'but' came butting in, no one wanted to swim in the pool. Then, suddenly, one young man appeared out of nowhere and accomplished the feat. The philanthropist was overjoyed. He ran to congratulate and garland the courageous man.

"Wait a minute," said the young man. "Before you shower me with gifts, I want to know who pushed me in!"

Life is like that. You will be pushed into it. Living is not the problem. It happens naturally. That young man swam naturally, didn't he? The trouble was what lay in the water, as he was swimming. There will be crocodiles like that in your life too. You may feel your boss is a crocodile or your mother-in-law or your husband or your colleague too.

You must learn to navigate through these odds. Only then will you be able to aim big and achieve big. In other words, the right balance of head and heart is a first step toward being a brilliant individual.

There are some things you should keep in mind that will help you on your way.

Keep Your 'Will' in a Positive State

The power of the human 'will' has long been endorsed as a formidable force of change in the world. If history is anything to go by, one man's achievement has changed the course of humanity forever. Look at the life of Mahatma Gandhi or Abraham Lincoln. See what they could accomplish through their will.

You must keep your 'will' in a positive state. If you are keeping yourself in a state of restlessness and in a state of in-gratitude, if you are taking your body for granted, then nothing you achieve or accomplish will suffice. All the wealth you acquire will seem like a trifle.

Void —
Receive —   Enlightenment
Think —
Believe —

Mystical Key

Contribution

Love / Enjoy \ Learn

You should be aware of which wealth you are acquiring, moment by moment. Develop the emotional will to witness the miracles of life. That is a wealth of a different kind.

Looking at Things in Totality

There is a principle of God-consciousness that is a sustaining factor everywhere. Develop the proper spiritual apparatus to realise this. Just as a dentist or a surgeon cannot look inside the body without the proper apparatus, so too individuals cannot look within and see the harmony that exists in all things, without proper spiritual apparatus.

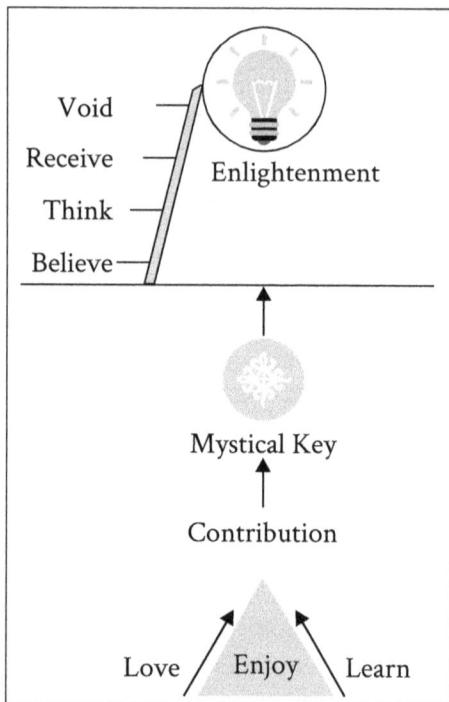

A very important part of this apparatus is the ability to look at things in their totality. There is beauty in everything. If you can see this, you will also see the harmony in all things. Then you will see that there is harmony in life's difficulties too. They are blessings of the Lord, bestowed at the right moment, to teach you important lessons. Just as a diamond gets polished when rough edges are smoothened through abrasion, so too, difficulties can polish you into a wonderful human being. When you look at things in their totality, you will realise this.

Increasing Your Awareness

If you do not increase your own awareness, then your quality of life will suffer, no matter what you have achieved. Unawareness brings about a dimension of invalidation. Take the example of technology. Great advancements have been achieved through technology; the internet has given humanity unprecedented access to knowledge.

However, if you delve deeper, despite all the knowledge at your fingertips, have you become more aware? Please note here, that technology is not being denounced at all. What is being highlighted is that, outward advancements do not necessarily reflect inner growth.

When you realise this, you will become aware of two things: you should work not merely being an outer winner in life, but also in becoming an inner winner of life.

The outer winner will achieve success, but someone who is also an inner winner will achieve something far more important: satisfaction. The ability to be satisfied is vital. Else, outer success will give you many comforts, and make you comfortably miserable.

Sage Vishwamitra transforming his life's journey from being a powerful king to attain the title of the best among sages, Brahmarshi, despite facing many obstacles, is yet another shining example of how one can 'Aim Big and Achieve Big.'

Excerpts from an interview with Warren Buffet, the second Richest man who has donated billions to charity.

Here are some very interesting aspects of his life:

1. He bought his first share at age 11 and he now regrets that he started too late!

2. He bought a small farm at age 14 with savings from delivering newspapers.

3. He still lives in the same small 3-bedroom house in mid-town Omaha, which he bought when he got married 50 years ago. He says that he has everything he needs in that house. His house does not have a fence.

4. He does not have security people around him.

5. He never travels by a private jet, although he owns the world's largest private jet company.

6. His company, Berkshire Hathaway, in turn owns 63 companies. He writes only one letter each year to the CEOs of these companies, giving them goals for the year. He never holds meetings or calls them on a regular basis. He has given his CEO's only two rules.

Rule number 1: do not lose any of your share holder's money.

Rule number 2: Do not forget rule number 1.

7. He does not socialise with the high society crowd. His past time after he gets home is to make himself some popcorn and watch Television.

8. Bill Gates, the world's richest man met him for the first time only 5 years ago. Bill Gates did not think he had anything in common with Warren Buffet. So he had scheduled his meeting only for 30 minutes. But when Gates met him, the meeting lasted for ten hours and Bill Gates became a Warren Buffet fan.

His advice to young people: Stay away from credit cards, invest in yourself and remember:

A: Money doesn't create man but it is man who created money.

B: Live your life as simple as you are.

C: Don't do what others say, just listen to them, but do what you feel good.

D: Don't go on brand name; just wear those things in which you feel comfortable.

E: Don't waste your money on unnecessary things; just spend on people who are really in need.

F: After all, it's your life, then why give a chance for others to rule.

The above may not make you Warren Buffet. However, it will surely make you successful and bring you more wisdom.

Reflection Point

When will you employ your spiritual key?

Do you believe in aiming big and achieving big?

Are you operating from the mindset 'I Can' rather than 'I Can't'?

Are you creative enough to deal with obstacles not from a victim pattern but from the victor pattern?

Destiny

There are two ways of looking at the question of destiny: one is that you create your own and the other is that your destiny is already written.

Many believe that we all have a date with our destiny, that we create our own. This is especially the case in the west. When we create our own destiny, the whole focus is to create our tomorrows. By creating our tomorrows, we are living for it.

The Indian approach, however, is that you cannot create destiny. Destiny happens. Whatever is written will happen, so whatever is in your destiny, take it as *prasada* (blessing).

Now let us look at the psychology in this. If you are creating your destiny, you are living for tomorrow and that tomorrow becomes your heaven. You will create a wonderful world... tomorrow. The trouble with this approach is that there is always another tomorrow waiting. There will never be an ending of this 'tomorrow'. So, your whole life is lived for tomorrow. And in this way, somewhere, the poetry of life is missed.

However, if you accept that 'this is my destiny', then your mind is not running for tomorrow. It is accepting the present. When you do that, you may not create a wonderful tomorrow, but you will be living a wonderful today. That 'today' happens every day. If you learn to live today properly, then every day becomes a pleasure. You will live your destiny.

> Then you will realise that 'today' carries your 'yesterday' and it carries your 'tomorrow'. Therefore, all time is 'now'.
>
> If you were miserable yesterday, then there are chances of you being miserable even today. The misery of your yesterday lands in the today. And if you are miserable today, your tomorrow is also going to be miserable.

Today carries your tomorrows and your yesterdays. Therefore, all time is now. Life happens only in today and that too 'here' and 'now'.

Is there any other way one can look at destiny? The question of destiny is always one of conflict.

Any conflict is a result of lack of clarity. This lack of clarity creates unnecessary expectations of what destiny might hold in store.

As mentioned above, if you approach a moment with fullness or joy, whatever destiny offers, you will meet that destiny with the fullness of joy. So why worry about one's destiny at all? A worrying mind, when faced with destiny, will continue to worry.

Another dimension of destiny is – whatever you have done in the past, there is a dimension that lands you in the present. This dimension is a mysterious one. So, destiny is a mystery.

Look at the life of Karna. He was never at peace with destiny. What happened to him was the result of his past. How did he relate to it in his lifetime, was it from wisdom or ignorance?

Reflect on this how to transform destiny into destination.

I recall one of the recent anecdotes that I heard.

I hired a plumber to help me carry out repairs at an old farmhouse. By the time he arrived, he had already gone through a rough and tiresome day.

A flat tire, his electric drill fault, his old car breaking down, his tiffin being spoilt, the loss of his wallet, the bank calling him for loan repayments...

With all tension and stress, he still finished my repairs satisfactorily.

Since his car broke down, I drove him home. While I drove him home, he sat silently, but I could sense his agony and restlessness.

On arriving at the destination, he invited me in to meet his family. As we walked towards the front door, he paused at a small tree, touching the tips of the branches with both hands and closed his eyes.

When the door opened, he was smiling and happy. Within seconds he underwent an amazing transformation.

He hugged his two small children, gave his wife a kiss, laughed, and never even slightly made them feel the troubles that he had encountered that day.

I was astonished, taken aback and curious. Seeing my inquisitive eyes he told, "Oh, that's my Trouble Tree. It is my best friend. It is my trouble carrier for the night".

He further added, "I know I can't help having troubles on the job, but one thing's for sure, those troubles don't belong in the house with my wife and the children. So I just hang them up on the tree every night when I come home and ask God to take care of them. Then, in the morning I pick them up again."

He smiled and shared a secret, "When I come out in the morning to pick them up, there aren't nearly as many as I remember hanging them there, the night before!"

Life may be a burden of worries, but there is a way to keep our loved ones untouched from these worries. In this process, he created space and surrendered to the unknown thereby learning the lesson of the art of detachment.

Time will heal every wound provided you bring quality of understanding to it.

Spreading smiles and happiness to our loved ones also, in turn, relieves us of the stress of the play of destiny.

Tough times don't last, but tough people do... as goes the saying.

Here is another tale from the mythology on the play of destiny.

There lived a poor Brahmin with his wife in a remote village. He had no children. His entire possession was a solitary horse. He was as attached to the horse as he may have been to his child. The villagers mocked his fondness for a horse to say least.

One day, the wandering sage Narada passed by his village. He met the Brahmin with his wife. Both of them took good care of the sage. They were poor and yet impressed him with their hospitality. The sage delved a little deeper into their destiny to figure out what was in store for them. He could decipher that at any given time the poor man could own only one horse. The sage went a little deeper with his destiny reading, for the poor Brahmin and realised that he could own many horses but at a given time only one horse would be by his side.

Sage Narada advised the poor Brahmin to sell his only horse and out of the proceeds educate a student in the study of Vedas, as teaching was his dharma, instead of being overtly attached to any horse. The poor Brahmin heeded to the advice and did what was told. The villagers were surprised at his act of giving up his love and attachment to the solitary horse. Thus, his teaching began.

Respecting his cause, a rich man from the village gave him another horse. After a while, the poor man sold that horse too and inducted another student. The neighbouring village head hearing this donated him another horse for his noble act of teaching... and fast forward... the cycle repeated and in the process, he educated many students in the village and in the neighbourhood.

His destiny was to have one horse at a time, yet he converted this to his destiny to teach many students. This was a creative way of dealing with destiny that changed him for better.

Reflection Point

Is there a half-truth situation around you? If so, which side are you looking at?

Qualities of a Wise Leader

Swamiji, recently, I made a career transition from the academics to head an organisation. I am aspiring to be the leader of many men and in a nutshell, can you enlighten me as to how to be a successful leader?

Learn from Life

One of the qualities of an enlightened person is that through proper and wise effort, she learns and discovers life. It is also important for you to imbibe the qualities of a wise person in your life. For example, consider our late president Abdul Kalam. He was an intellectual powerhouse, and yet, in his life, he never dominated anyone. Have you seen how certain intellectuals dominate others with their intellect? Abdul Kalam never did this.

When asked the question of his religion, Kalam said, "My religion is the discipline of learning." He had the discipline of learning. Learn from life... learn from your colleagues.

What is true learning? What is the difference between learning and collecting the garbage of knowledge? How should we learn? Lord Krishna says learn from failures and successes, through meeting people. When you begin to do this, experiencing the growing of egoless-ness becomes beautiful.

Abdul Kalam had extraordinary eyes while seeing ordinary things. Most of you are so busy you do not see that life is your greatest master.

> **"**
>
> If you do not see God in life, you miss life in your attempt to see God. So, open your eyes and then see.
>
> If in your own family you do not see angels, then you have missed seeing the beauty and the benediction of life. Thus, with such eyes, look at life. **"**

A successful leader should focus on mastering the following attributes:

◆ Self-Transformation.

◆ Respect limitations and go beyond.

◆ Shared vision in a team.

◆ Interconnectedness among the stakeholders.

◆ Encourage team learning.

◆ Ensure team synergy to the aligned goal.

◆ Manage success and failure.

A leader is one who manages both success and failure.

When the rocket project failed, Abdul Kalam's guru and leader Prof. Satish Dhawan said, "I will handle the press." This was despite Abdul Kalam being in charge of the first experimental rocket 'Rohini Technology Payload'.

Prof. Satish Dhawan told the press that though his team had failed, they would succeed the next time. "We failed! But I have very good trust in my team that the next time we shall succeed for sure," and made everyone to believe in the team.

In the very next year, the same team led by Dr. Kalam successfully launched Rohini RS-1 into the orbit! The whole country was proud and cheering the success of the launch.

Prof. Satish Dhawan congratulated Dr. Kalam and his team for their feat. He further insisted that Dr. Kalam conduct the press conference that day!

A good leader is one who takes the responsibility of failure but passes on the glory of success to others.

When you follow some of these simple qualities, you live a simple life. By doing so, you learn not to demonstrate the drama of your foolish knowledge. And this is the essence of a true leader.

Here is a narrative from Indian mythology on the life of Sage Dattatreya. He learnt from 24 gurus. The following are some of his gurus.

- The earth represents acceptance, forbearance and benevolence.

- The wind symbolises freedom of movement. Being always on the move, and never attached to anything. It symbolises the quality of touch and go.

- The sun, moon and the ocean emphasise the unchanging nature of truth.

- The sky shows the infinite nature of the self and quality of being detached, yet open to multiple possibilities in life.

- The spider reminds us of the transient nature of this material world.

- The moth, elephant, deer and fish warn us against the overwhelming distractions caused by desires.

- The pigeon, honeybee, kurari bird and pingala warn us against worldly attachments.

- The child evokes in us the happiness of freedom from material care.

- The python and honeybee emphasise the benefits of simple living.

- The fire and water teach the power to purify the contamination of material world.

- The maiden and snake teach us how to avoid any distraction caused by unwanted things.

- The arrowsmith teaches us to remain focused and concentrate on the goal.

- The caterpillar teaches us that by concentrating on God, one can return to Godhead, the ultimate goal.

These are among the most inspiring insights on leadership.

Reflection Point

Is the message fully internalised, imbibed and assimilated?

Is there a sufficiency of leaders to learn from as in the case of Dattatreya?

Are you on the path of continuous search for leadership qualities in you?

Be Wary of Ego in Your Journey

What makes ego such a deadly poison that the noblest are also affected by its pranks? How can one recognise it and deal with it?

It is said that all most all noble souls of Indian mythology were swayed by the thunder of the ego... in some way or the other, at some time or another in their lives.

A journalist interviewing a socialist leader asks, "If you had two Mercedes Benz cars, what would you do?"

The socialist answers, "I would keep one and give one to the poor."

"If you had two bungalows?"

"I would keep one and give one to the poor."

"If you had ten lakhs of money?"

"I would keep five and give five to the poor."

The questioning continues in this manner.

There were two hens in the socialist's house. The journalist asks him, "What about these two hens? Will you give one away to the poor?"

The socialist replies, "I will not give these hens to anybody. All those other things were not yet mine, so I didn't mind dividing them. But these hens are mine, so I will not divide them."

See how the ego works? It is very sly. In life, you can be street smart, but not wise. The ego makes you smart, but not wise. And therefore, you suffer from the great heat of struggle. In my experience, many egoistic people are smart at making money but they are not necessarily wise. Therefore, you suffer this way.

Can you address this ego that makes you smart, but not wise?

In the corporate world, you find stress and chaos cannot be solved by street smartness but only can be solved with wisdom.

Let us reflect on the episode from Mahabharata.

Arjuna had gone to the Himalayas in the quest of divine weapons from Indra.

In case of war, he had to face invincible warriors like Bhishma, Drona, Kripa, Ashwatthama, Karna and many such others. For this, it was necessary to acquire more power. The other four Pandavas and Draupadi found life devoid of joy in his absence. Desiring a change of scene, they moved on in search of a more peaceful place in the forest during their exile.

At last, they came to the Narayanasrama forest. They decided to take rest and stay there for a while. One day, the north-east wind blew over a flower near Draupadi. The sweet scent of the flower charmed her.

Draupadi felt a deep desire to possess that flower known as Saugandhika. She requested Bhima to get her that flower. She was very insistent.

Bhima was only too pleased to satisfy even the smallest of her desires. He instantly set out in the direction from which the fragrance came. The way through the forest was far from easy.

Before long at the foot of a mountain, he saw a huge monkey resting on his path, blocking the way. He asked the monkey to get up and clear the way for him. The monkey was in no mood to oblige.

It said, "I am too old and weak to move. You can jump over me." Proud Bhima, incensed by this audacity, again asked the monkey to move. He said, "You old monkey, you don't know who you are talking to. I am a Kshatriya from the Kuru clan. I am the son of Kunti and the Wind God. I am Bhima, brother of the famous Hanuman. So, if you offend me through any further resistance, you will incur my wrath. I command you to better get up and move aside without wasting my time. "

The monkey said, "If you are in such hurry, you can move my tail aside and go ahead." Bhima's threats did not have any effect on the monkey. Instead, it asked,"Who is Hanuman? Tell me what is so great about him? What did he do?"

Bhima told him, "How can you be so silly and ignorant? Have you not heard of the mighty Hanuman who jumped over to Lanka, across the sea, one hundred yojanas wide, to find Sita, Rama's wife? Indeed you are ignorant."

The monkey only smiled. Finding no other way, Bhīma tried to pull the monkey's tail aside. But he could not move it even a little bit. He put all his might in the endeavour, but to no avail. He was all perspiration. Despite his best efforts, he could not move the tail. As such the question of challenging this monkey for a show of strength did not arise. He felt very humiliated and subdued. He told the monkey, "You are no ordinary monkey. Please tell me who you are. I accept defeat and bow to you."

The monkey said, "Bhima, I am that Hanuman – the name you mentioned a little while ago. I am your brother. Your path ahead is perilous. It is the path of the deities and is not safe for men. So I came to caution you. I knew you have come to collect the Saugandhika flower. I shall show you the pond, where this flower grows. You can collect as many as you want and go back."

Bhima was happy. He bowed to Hanuman and requested him to show his huge form in which he jumped over the sea, one hundred yojanas wide, to land on Lanka. Hanuman increased his size till he seemed to occupy the whole landscape, like a hill. His form was dazzlingly white; so Bhima had to cover his eyes. Resuming his normal form, Hanuman embraced Bhima and blessed him. He also assured him, "When you roar like a lion on the battlefield, my voice shall join yours and strike terror in the hearts of your enemies."

"I will be there on the flag of the chariot of Arjuna. You will be victorious." With Hanuman's embrace, Bhima's strength had also increased. Hanuman wanted to free his brother Bhima from his ego and to give him the greater strength to fight his enemies."

Hanuman then took leave of his brother after blessing him. Following Hanuman's advice, Bhima collected many Saugandhika flowers from the pond and went back to present them to Draupadi, who was anxiously waiting for his return.

Reflection Point

Will you employ a spiritual key when faced with testing times and when your ego surfaces?

It is indeed a mystery as to how ego enters even noble souls. Be wary of both passive ego and aggressive ego... both are sure to lead you to doom.

How many times have you caught your ego playing pranks on you?

Change Your Thought and Your Stars Will Change you

The Chairman of a bank recently asked me, "We work in a highly systematised world where all practices are well laid out. All that people have to do is follow a set system. How can new thinking be expected from them and how do we foster a spirit of new thinking in them?

I started my reply with an anecdote.

What is the size of God?

A boy asked his father: What's the size of God?

The father looked up at the sky and seeing an aeroplane asked the son: What's the size of that aeroplane?

The boy answered: It's very small. I can barely see it.

The father then took him to the airport and as they approached an aeroplane he asked: And now, what is the size of this one?

The boy answered: Wow daddy, this is huge!

Then the father told him: God, is like this, His size depends on the distance between you and Him. The closer you are to Him, the greater He will be in your life!

So too in an organisation, however systematised its processes may be, when one has a closer view of the objects, new dimensions open up in the approaches to everything from people to process and the product itself.

A village maiden pounding rice in the traditional way would hardly be noticed by most of us. To the enlightened mind of Dattatreya, however, she was a lesson, to be remembered. The great sage was walking in his village one day when he saw a beautiful maiden pounding rice. She was wearing lots of bangles that clinked together noisily as she went about her work. As her master was sleeping inside and she did not wish to disturb him by the noise, she started to remove one bangle at a time in order to reduce the noise level. She removed them, one by one, until there was only one bangle left. This one bangle made no noise.

What did Dattatreya learn?

Our mind is like the bangles of the beautiful maiden. Our thoughts rattle and clang noisily each day. While we work, our minds are filled with so many things, like the many bangles of the woman. We should remove those myriad thoughts like she removed her bangles until we are only left with one focus alone: the work with which we are occupied.

Therefore, a single bangle represents single thought. This focused thought does not create noise like many bangles held together while pounding rice. Thus, a focused single thought reflects the silent mind.

How many of you have learnt to keep your mind focused? With a firm resolve, just focus on doing whatever you are doing. Often, you do not do this.

Your mind has many branches and travels at lightning speed in many directions. With this external speed and internal noise, you are not able to digest an experience. When you are not able to digest an experience, you will not be able to tap into the message and poetry and benediction of the experience. Therefore, you find that, when the final moment approaches, you have neither experienced life nor really lived it. Life passes and you feel something is missing.

Why be afraid of what is happening in life?

Please reflect on this episode that I heard recently.

At the point of death, a man, Tom Smith, called his children and he advised them to follow his footsteps so that they could have peace of mind in all that they did.

His daughter, Sara said, "Daddy, it is unfortunate that you are dying without a penny in your bank. Other fathers that you tag as being corrupt, thieves of public funds left houses and properties for their children; even this house that we live in is a rented apartment. Sorry, I can't emulate you, just go, let's chart our own course."

A few moments later, their father gave up the spirit and joined the creator.

Three years later, Sara went for an interview in a multinational company. At the interview, the Chairman of the committee asked, "Which Smith are you?"

Sara replied, "I am Sara Smith. My Dad Tom Smith is now no more."

Chairman cut in, "O my God! Are you Tom Smith's daughter?" He turned to the other members and said, "This Smith was the one who signed my membership form into the Institute of Administrators and his recommendation earned me where I am today. He did all these free. I didn't even know his address, he never knew me. He just did it for me."

He turned to Sara, "I have no questions for you, consider yourself as having got this job, come tomorrow, your letter will be waiting for you."

Sara Smith became the Corporate Affairs Manager of the company with two cars with drivers, a duplex attached to the office, and a salary of £1,00,000 per month...

After two years of working for the company, the MD of the company came from America to announce that he'd be resigning and needed a replacement. A personality with high integrity was sought after, again the company's Consultant nominated Sara Smith. In an interview, she was asked the secret of her success.

With tears in her eyes, she replied, "My Daddy paved the way for me. It was after he died that I knew he was financially poor but strikingly rich in integrity, discipline and honesty."

She was asked again, why she was weeping as she was no longer a kid to miss her dad after such a long absence. She replied, "At the point of death, I insulted my dad for being a man of integrity. I hope he will forgive me in his grave now. I didn't work for all these; he did it for me to just walk into it."

So, finally, she was asked, "Will you follow your father's footsteps as he requested?"

And her simple answer was, "I now adore the man, I have a big picture of him in my living room and at the entrance of my house. He deserves all credit for whatever I have achieved in life."

Are you like Tom Smith?

चम्पकपटवासनान्यायः

The maxim of the champaka flower in the cloth.

The champaka flower leaves its fragrance in the piece of cloth in which it is kept, even after the flower is taken away.

The maxim is used to denote that the virtues of a man continue to exercise their genial influence upon others even after the man has departed from this world.

It pays to build a name, the reward doesn't come quickly but it will come however long it may take and it lasts longer.

Integrity, discipline, self-control and the love of God make a person wealthy, not a fat bank account. Leave a good heritage.

Reflection Point

Can you be a light unto yourself?

Can you express gratitude to all those who have helped you?

Do you possess a high degree of integrity in testing times?

Is it understood that the reach of integrity will take one far... in leaving a legacy behind?

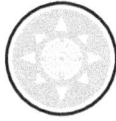

The Form and the Formless

"We are in a constant search mode outside of us. Is there wisdom to search within ourselves? I find myself suffocated and lonely in spite of my stupendous worldly successes. Is there a way out? What will one realise when one begins the search within?" I was asked this question recently in a corporate gathering.

Your journey within will take you from the gross to the subtle. The 'gross' body is the physical body that you identify with: heart, brain, liver, kidneys, lungs etc.

Delve deeper within, and you will see that there is something intangible to you, something finer than the body; these are your thoughts. Look even further and you will see something subtler than thoughts: feelings. Going beyond that, there is something even more subtle than your feelings: your values. You will see that with certain values come feelings, from these feelings, thoughts emerge and from thoughts, actions result.

Therefore, an object has a form, your body has a form but your thought form is subtler and your feelings even more so. Your values are almost formless. Take music, for instance; music has a certain form but, the feeling that a *raag* creates has no form at all. If you go even further, your values are triggered by beliefs. Beyond these beliefs, there is somebody who is witnessing all this. Somebody is witnessing as a witness (*Sakshi)* to all this. If you can come in touch with that witness, a spiritual awakening happens.

Being a *Sakshi* or witness leads you to the cosmic consciousness. It is only in the experience of witnessing consciousness that goes beyond ego, that you can experience cosmic consciousness. Hence witnessing consciousness is the door to cosmic consciousness.

But why most of you are impatient? Have you thought about it? Why are you impatient? It is because your mind is always bent on acquiring things. You want to acquire wealth, power, sexual pleasure, name, fame etc. Is not the story of your life always in the acquiring? There is always much more to acquire than what you have acquired. So, the mind gets bored with what you have acquired and becomes restless in the process of acquiring. With such a bored and restless mind, you naturally seek an escape from boredom.

Try not to get lost in acquiring, but also do see the poetry and richness in 'what is'. In that space, you can acquire. Then acquiring adds to the richness. Right now, you are acquiring out of boredom and ego. Such acquisition is adding to boredom.

I have a friend who is an expert flirt. He has a way with women and the women, though they know he is a flirt, they too flirt with him. He said to me, very interestingly, "Swamiji, I have had so many affairs, but I am bored with them." Then he said, "Swamiji, meditation is the only way because, in meditation, you see the richness of what is." In flirting, there is an excitement to acquire, thereafter boredom sets in. In meditation, you see 'what is'. You see the richness.

Friends, when you can see the richness of 'what is', and out of that richness go about acquiring things such as money or getting married, then your marriage will add to the richness because you will see the richness in your wife too. If you are bored and get married, you will get bored with your wife.

How is patience applicable to the corporate world? Should you not be restless till a goal or task is achieved? Impatience with certain things help you to go after them passionately, doesn't it?

You have to see the foolishness of such thinking that restlessness leads to passion. Look at it from another angle. It is commitment that leads you to passion. When commitment leads to passion, there is an energy of creativity and enthusiasm that leads to wellness whereas restlessness will only induce more stress, not wellness. What is the use of such achievements?

Look at the way of life. For a plant, you have to give time for it to turn into a tree; a child - you have to wait till it turns into an adult; for a singer, time is required to rise to greatness. So patience is the very foundation of your life. If you have patience you will fish where there are fishes, else, you will be fishing restlessly where there are no fishes.

Let us reflect on this episode from Ramayana.

King Vali was very brave and courageous. Before dawn, he used to go from the East coast of the sea to the West coast, to pay his homage to the sun-god, Surya. He was so brave and powerful that on his way to pay homage to Surya, he used to toss the mountain peaks upward and catch them like they were balls. After completing the tedious task of paying homage to the sun-god in all the four directions, he used to return to Kishkindha without even being tired.

Vali was the husband of Tara, who was an Apsara. As mythology states, fourteen types of gems or treasures were produced from the churning of the ocean. One gem is that various Apsaras (divine nymphs) were produced and Tara was an Apsara produced from the churning of the ocean. Vali who was with the devas, helping them in the churning of the ocean, married Tara.

Wandering in the forest with his brother Lakshmana in search of his wife Sita, who was kidnapped by the demon king Ravana, Lord Rama met the demon Kabandha and killed him, freeing him from a curse. The freed Kabandha advised Lord Rama to seek the help of Sugriva to find Sita.

Continuing on his journey, Lord Rama met Hanuman and was impressed by his intelligence and skills as an orator. Hanuman introduced Lord Rama and Lakshmana to Sugriva. Sugriva narrated the entire story of how Vali became his enemy. Vali misunderstood him being left alone in a cave by Sugriva, conned by a trick of asura that Vali was dead, and closed the entry of the cave so that the asura enemies did not reach him.

Emerging from the cave, Vali dethroned Sugriva and forcefully took his wife. He made her his second wife, much to her resentment. Sugriva narrated to Lord Rama how he was entirely innocent.

Sugriva was very scared of Vali and was full of doubts if Lord Rama could kill him. He told Lord Rama, many incredible stories of Vali's valour. As a proof, he showed Lord Rama a hole in a sal tree which Vali had made in one shot. When it was Lord Rama's turn, he penetrated 7 trees of sal in a row with a single arrow. After going through the trees, the arrow even struck a huge rock and shattered it into pieces. Sugriva was happy and said, "O Rama, you are great."

Lord Rama asked Sugriva to challenge Vali and bring him outside Kishkindha. As Lord Rama explained later, for 14 years he was not allowed to enter any city. Moreover, Lord Rama did not want any unnecessary bloodbath of Vali's army with whom he wanted to maintain friendly relations. Despite this, killing Vali would not be possible for Lord Rama as Sugriva and Vali were identical twins.

Sugriva assured Lord Rama in return for his help that he and his army would help in defeating Ravana and rescuing Sita. Sugriva challenged Vali to a fight. When Vali charged forth to meet the challenge, Lord Rama emerged from the forest and killed him with an arrow from the back of a tree.

A dying Vali told Lord Rama, "If you are searching for your wife you should have come to me for help and friendship. Whoever took Sita, be it Ravana himself, I would have defeated him and would have brought him to your feet, to your mercy."

Vali while dying asked the following questions:

Sugriva now made my wife a widow and is about to snatch my kingdom. What was my crime?

Even if I committed a crime (with my brother), what is your right to kill me? I would have helped you in getting Sita, your father king Dasharatha helped my father to fight against demons.

Lord Rama responded to Vali as under:-

The younger brother should be treated like a son. Even if he made a mistake you should forgive him, especially when he promised to respect you for your whole life.

About his authority, he said he had permission from King Bharata to spread righteousness and punish evils. And there you are being punished.

You are one who has not followed the path of dharma, hence you don't have a right to speak on it.

If you are blessed with a boon of taking half of the strength of a person in front of you in a combat, such talent has to be used, not abused. The very fact you abused by taking away your brother's wife, you are in adharma.

The chaos that your brother has gone through – not listening to him or your own wife, is it dharma?

Your arrogance did not allow you to see the truth. Hence, such a warfare or rananeeti was adopted to hit you from the back.

In *dharma* (righteousness) there are two cases... one is *samanya (ordinary)* and other is *vishesha (extra-ordinary)* – that is the strategy of warfare that Lord Rama adopted.

As a part of warfare strategy, if the person has the power to take away half the strength of his opponent in a combat, it is a right strategy to hit him from behind.

Reflection Point

Is there a prayerful pause, prayerful shock and prayerful direction in your day?

Recount instances of you resolving a complex issue by being a witnessing consciousness?

As a spiritual exercise, practice seeing form and formlessness in all that you see.

Yoga – A Path of Self Realisation

> Striving for a healthier, happier life, we would, at some stage or the other, realise that spirituality is important too, in our quest. Spirituality, largely means a system of belief or state of consciousness, focused on self-realisation. All human experience is lived through the paradigm of this individual 'self', the entity that we have come to identify ourselves with. It is therefore imperative for us to understand the true nature of this 'self'.

A life rooted in such a quest for realisation and its attainment can bring us untold joy, not in the distant future, but in the only facet of time that is or ever will be important – the present moment.

So how does one go about attaining self-realisation, and thereby, happiness?

Hindu thought, which has for centuries examined this and many other existential questions provide the answer through three important pillars: *tantra, yoga* and *Vedanta*. Of these three pillars, yoga has been the most recognised, around the world. Though the word 'yoga' may be popular, there is a science behind it that has not yet become as widespread as the *asanas* or postures with which it has become strongly associated.

In this series, we will examine the true meaning of yoga and the most scientific and logical way in which it can lead us to self-realisation.

Quintessentially, yoga is the joining of the lower self to the higher self, the joining of the earth to heaven. In fact, all the three pillars of Hindu thought are methods to join earth to heaven; heaven not as a distance, place or geography, but as a state of consciousness.

Among the greatest contributions to yoga are the concise aphorisms from the great Patanjali's yoga *sutras*. Patanjali's contribution is called *ashtanga* yoga. It constitutes the 8 limbs of yoga, in which *asana* (postures) and *pranayama* (breathing exercises) form the 3rd and 4th limbs. These are the types of yoga practised most in the modern day. What many people call by the general name of 'yoga' today, is in fact, a branch of *ashtanga* yoga called *hatha* yoga. It is in *hatha yoga pradipika* that we find all the different *asanas* as they are practised today. It is sad to note that today, many people do the *asanas* of yoga for the purposes of staying fit or looking good. But yoga goes beyond this. It is also about 'feeling good' and 'being good.'

While the great *rishis* and gurus of our ancient country gave us many a signpost on the path of self-realisation, the sheer profundity of their insights is often beyond the grasp of the common man. Uncovering the truth, they spoke so that we may benefit from it, requiring another very important element: the omniscience of a self-realised guru. The clear mind and intellectual perception of a guru can simplify complex ideas and concepts. If material existence is the darkness through which we must navigate our way to self-realisation, the guru is the light that leads the way.

In ancient days, a guru's ashram was not easily accessible to spiritual seekers. They used to be in the mountains or forests, somewhere far away. The rationale is that there should be thirst within the seekers. Only then will they be able to understand the guru. There are then students who, despite difficulties, navigate their way through, and show their sincerity to learn, to seek and to understand. These are the fit beings to receive the knowledge of enlightenment.

Lord Krishna says in the revered Bhagavad Gita, that we can understand only by bowing down to the guru, by asking healthy questions and by doing *seva* or services of goodness. Only then the guru may teach. He may try to teach before that, but the student may not understand.

Therefore, in summary, as we go through life, in search of happiness, we must all, come to the path of spirituality, where sooner or later, the quest and need for an understanding of the self and, eventually, of self-realisation becomes apparent. Of the three-fold path provided by Hindu thought, yoga, is one. Essentially, it is the joining of the lower self to the higher self. Walking this path requires two things: firstly, that the way is lit by the wisdom of a guru and secondly, that we are ready for the reception of profound knowledge. To make ourselves ready, we must: learn to acknowledge the guru and bow down to him, ask healthy questions and engage ourselves through services of goodness.

Reflection Point

Have you discovered a thirsty seeker in you? If yes, who is your Guru?

Or, are you lost in spiritual shopping for finding a Guru?

How Yoga Transforms

Transformation occurs when you approach life's situations in a different way vis-à-vis what you have done before. It leads you to decide differently and choose prudently. The decisions and choices are the outward indicators of your inner changes.

Therefore, let us look at your decision-making processes, whether you do it subconsciously within yourselves or externally, at the organisational level. Decision making starts with the analysis to decipher what is right and what is wrong. This sense of 'right' and 'wrong' could have moral, personal, professional, financial, familial or any other parameters influencing it. The analysis should lead to a conceptual change, which re-looks at these important parameters. This conceptual change, often a shift in paradigm, results in a directional change. The directional change then leads to a behavioural change i.e. a change in the way you act and react to challenges that confront you.

To put it in simpler terms, your actions often result from your belief systems: as is the belief, so is the thought and as is the thought, so is the action.

And, it is this very belief system which constitutes your core, that yoga transforms. It changes the habit patterns of the mind by changing the core of your beliefs. In the process, it changes your thoughts and your actions. Yoga brings about a conceptual change and then a behavioural change, leading to an experience.

Recently, someone narrated this example. Reflect on this.

Asha went to school in her neighbouring village, where, she wasn't well known.

For three weeks, she was late to school, and each time, the teacher punished her for that.

In the fourth week, Asha did not attend school at all and many thought she had given up on school on account of the daily punishment.

However, in the fifth week, Asha reported again and this time she was in class, earlier than everyone else.

When the teacher came to class, Asha was punished for not attending school in the previous week. But, the teacher was also kind enough to praise her for coming early that day, stating that the punishments had finally yielded some results.

Just then, Asha asked if she could say something and the teacher gave her permission.

"I've been raised up by a single mother without a brother or a sister. Five weeks ago, my mother fell ill and was hospitalised. The three weeks I came late, I had to prepare something for her every morning and pass by the hospital to deliver the same. Unfortunately, my mother passed away last week and that's the reason I did not come to school. We buried her last Sunday. Today, I came early since I didn't have to prepare anything or even pass by the hospital. And now that she is gone, I will always be early to school."

As she sat down, none in the whole class was able to hold back his / her tears; the teacher was not spared either.

How many times do you judge others for things that you know not?

Do you attempt to understand their situation or do you just judge from the case scenarios?

Some situations are not relative and what you think, could be very far removed from the truth.

Don't assume you know what others go through or that people move in the same pace or direction as you.

Life is far from that.

Just be kind enough to love one another as God has commanded, take time and kindly find out why your friend has not been calling you or, why your messages are not being responded to promptly, or, why someone has been missing from your midst – may be a colleague, friend, brother or sister, or even, why someone is always late.

Mastery	Psychological Silence	Daily Activity with Acuity
↓	↓	↓
Draw Energy from the Rising Sun	Keep your sorrow in silence	The warrior prepares his cup of tea

Keep your sorrow in psychological silence - whatever be the sorrow you experience, you should place it in silence... in a calm mind. This is a great discipline.

Draw your energy from the rising Sun – meaning always draw energy from the enlightened masters; do not draw energy from sorrow.

And a warrior prepares his cup of tea – meaning do your daily activities with acumen.

Reflection Point

Is there a half-truth situation like this? If so, which side are you looking at?

What Asanas Teach us

Buddha said life is full of misery. Not that life itself is misery, but rather, the way we live makes us feel miserable. We are always running from one situation to another.

In our search for happiness, we move through experiences, constantly hoping for fulfilment. This outward journey often leads to frustration, because once the experiences end, so does the fulfilment that they give us. Even successful people face frustration.

Have you noticed how money and popularity do not guarantee a person's happiness? Frustration not treated properly can lead to depression.

It is not the sensation of an experience that gives us joy, nor money nor power nor familial relationships. None of these gives us peace or joy. It is only when we realise that we wish to enter the world of yoga, does the realisation of true happiness begin. When we enter with such a willingness to learn, we should also enter with the willingness to unlearn what we already know. Often, we digress from what we know.

Let us understand the role of the postures or *asanas*, how they represent life and what they teach us.

If life is a ritual and a ceremony, we all have to take a position – a husband, a wife, a son, a child. The position we take is akin to a posture or *asana*. Yoga teaches us to find happiness even in a difficult posture. And it teaches us to experience the present moment, in all its fullness. Therefore, experiencing the fullness of the moment, we learn to find happiness in it.

Seek happiness, even in the difficult positions of life and when you seek, you will find it. You should learn to be in a state of *sukha* or happiness constantly. You will then realise that it is the energy of happiness that gets created in the posture or position of life. This energy of happiness can only be experienced in the present moment; not in the past, or the future.

When you apply proper and adequate effort, there will come a time when your postures in yoga and your efforts to find happiness in any position of life will become effortless. There is a flow to your *asanas* and your life. What do I mean by this? Consider, for instance, car driving. Initially, when you drive a car, you have to concentrate a lot. With time and adequate practice, however, car driving becomes effortless, even though there is still, technically, an effort being applied by you to drive. Your eyes see effortlessly, your body functions effortlessly, though there is still an effort being put into it. It is the same with happiness and joy. If you train yourself to find happiness in life, in the most difficult and the simplest of positions, and you learn to experience the fullness of each moment in its entirety, then there will come a time when happiness becomes effortless.

In summary, if life is a ceremony, connecting earth to heaven, then each position in your life is an *asana* or posture, and in every *asana*, if you can find that true happiness and joy, then, your very presence becomes a mantra.

Reflect on this.

When I was small I'd put my arms in my shirt and tell people that I had lost my arms.

Had that one pen with four colours and tried to push all the buttons at once.

Waited behind a door to scare someone, and then left as they took too long to come out.

Faked being asleep, so that I could be carried to bed.

Used to think that the moon followed our car.

Tried to balance the switch between 'On/Off'.

Was watching two drops of rain roll down the window and pretending that it was a race.

The only thing I had to take care of, was a school bag.

Swallowed a fruit seed and I was scared to death that a tree was going to grow in my tummy.

Closed the fridge extremely slowly to see when the lights went off.

Walked into a room, forgot what I needed, walked out, and then remembered.

Remember that when we were kids, we couldn't wait to grow up? And now we think why did we even grow up?

Childhood was the best part of our life.

I know you have a smile on your face while reading this...if you want someone close to you to smile too...go ahead and share these joyful memories.

Finally, I found the answer to the most asked question in my childhood.

What do you want to become when you grow up?

A child again.

Reflection Point

Can you be a light unto yourself to find happiness and joy?

How Yoga Changes
the Habit Patterns of the Mind

The mind usually dwells in lies. It does not wish to live in truth. Every *asana* teaches you to see the richness of the moment. It is because you are not able to see this, that you are forever living either in the future or the past. It is also because of this, that negative emotions such as jealousy, anger etc., arise. You are unable to see the beauty of the moment and so try to covet what others have.

Each of the *asanas*, representing a part of nature, teaches you something. Take for instance the posture of the cobra. The majestic cobra has the capacity to shed its skin when the time comes and grow new skin yet again. Do you have the capacity to drop yourself? The quality of the cobra you must introspect. Feel the joy of the change. Feel. Feel.

When you experience the richness of the feeling of joy, the mind learns to dwell in that change. Because the mind is not able to understand the richness of the moment, it yearns for the future. It is the same with negative emotions of jealousy and unhappiness, anger, and frustration. These are all due to the mind's inability to appreciate the joy of the moment.

Such a mind is noisy. Noisy and unable to enjoy the present moment, it cannot digest any experience to its fullest. Such undigested experiences are the root causes of unhappiness and sorrow. In an *asana*, you are digesting the moment. You are learning to do this. *Asanas* enable you to experience the moment, to celebrate the richness of the moment.

Let us examine how the mind works normally. An impulse falls on the mind. What is the mind? It is nothing but thought. Thought has a natural connection with memory. One memory will log on to another unhappy memory of the past. This unhappy memory will log on to more of the same and so on, to create an almost tsunami-like effect. And that becomes your pain centre.

POLLUTED ⟳ State ⟳ ENLIGHTENED

This is where yoga breaks the pattern. In yoga, when an impulse arises in the mind, the mind begins to understand it with a learning model: how to discover *stirasukhasana*, the posture of joy at the moment. You are not opening the memory files in your pain centre, making unnecessary connections with the past. You are instead, in a learning model. This learning model directs it to yoga.

This narration touched me most. Reflect deeply on this.

A very poor man lived with his wife.

One day, his wife, who had very long hair, asked him to buy her a comb for her hair to grow well and to be well-groomed.

The man felt very sorry as he had to say no to the request. He explained that he did not have money to even fix the strap of his watch that he had just broken.

She did not insist on her request.

The man went to work and passed by a watch shop, sold his damaged watch at a low price and went to buy a comb for his wife.

He came home in the evening with the comb in his hand ready to give to his wife.

He was surprised when he saw his wife with a very short cropped hair.

She had sold her hair and was holding a new watch strap in hand.

Tears flowed simultaneously from their eyes, not for the futility of their actions, but for the reciprocity of their love.

To love is nothing, to be loved is something but to love and to be loved by the one you love, that's Everything.

Never take love for granted.

Reflection Point

Will you employ your spiritual key to bring forth and receive love?

Values of Yoga

Yoga is an eight-fold path to nirvana. The parts of that eight-fold path are *yama, niyama, asana, pranayama, prathyahara, dharana, dhyana* and *samadhi.* We have hitherto discussed the most recognised part of this eight-fold path: *asana. Yama* and *niyama,* which make up the first and second parts, form the moral backbone of yoga. They mean, respectively, universal morality and personal observances that should be followed. Essentially they are the foundation of yoga.

Let us now look further into *yama,* universal morality. The *yamas* are broken down into five 'wise characteristics'; these are values we must cultivate within us.

The first yama is *ahimsa*: non-injury

It means do not be cruel to any living creature or hurt anyone. Look at life carefully. You will realise that at every moment, you are injuring yourself. If someone says something that you find unpleasant, you get hurt. If someone disagrees with you, if your spouse has different opinions from you, you get hurt. You are constantly getting hurt. In your upsets, in your anger, in your jealousy, in your frustrations you are injuring yourself. And when injuring yourself, please understand that your mind gets injured and emotions get injured too. This mental and emotional injury falls on the body and the body becomes diseased. 'When ease is disturbed, disease results'.

The second value is *satya* or truth

Living a truthful life is important. If you are a practitioner of yoga, you must learn to live a truthful life. Yet you must also be careful in the speaking of this truth. There are three types of speech. It is one of the professed values of the Indian system – s*atyam vada* - meaning utter the truth, *priyam vada* - meaning speak what is pleasant and *hitam vada* - meaning speak what is good and appropriate. Truth not only pertains to what you say truthfully, but also, to the effort to discover the truth.

How you speak it, what you say, how it would affect others are all things that should be considered.

Asteya is another core value

It means non-covetousness. What is not yours, do not take. When you are not coveting another's wife or possessions, you are able to give yourself completely to the moment. When you can renounce coveting, your total energy is in that moment and then your capacity to be with 'what is' increases.

Brahmacharya stands for sense control

Brahmacharya means abstinence, especially concerning sexual activity. It also means sexual mastery or celibacy. Celibacy is the result of an inner order. It is not the starting point. Hence *brahmacharya* is called the *brahmani charanti iti brahmacharya* - i.e. one who revels in *Brahma*. *Brahma* stands for fullness and purity.

The result of you being in purity and fullness is *brahmacharya*. Hence it is the ultimate end... it is not merely sexual control but sexual mastery.

Aparigraha stands for non-possessiveness

Aparigraha means not being greedy and being non-attached. It indicates to take only what is necessary and nothing more. And learn to let go of worldly attachments that entangle you further in the material world.

There is an analogy in Indian culture which promotes this aspect as a part of conserving Mother Nature. There is *Angakara Vritti*, where one burns a forest to get few loads of coal, *Malakara Vritti*, where one works for oneself and also for others and *Madhukara Vritti*, where one takes very little for oneself just the same as how a honey bee strives but leaves behind a honeycomb for others.

Why is it important to cultivate these values or wise characteristics? Once you have a value, the value will create its own pathway. For example, if you have a value that says you must make money, then the mind will begin to work in that way. Similarly, if you have values which say, 'I should be truthful, compassionate, generous, peaceful and without greed or possessiveness', then your mind will work towards those goals, either consciously or subconsciously.

Examine your organisation's core values and see if:

- you are aligned with it.
- you have missing links.
- you bridge the gap in the organisation as a leader.
- you constantly empower yourself and also, measure yourself against set values.

Hanuman is viewed as the ideal combination of "strength, heroic initiative and assertive excellence" and "loving and devoted to Lord Rama" as Shakti and Bhakti. He has been the patron deity of martial arts such as wrestling, acrobatics, as well as meditation and diligent scholarship. He symbolises the human excellences of inner self-control, faith and service to a cause, hidden behind the first impressions of a being that looks like a monkey.

It is said that Hanuman was the only one who had mastered nine forms of traditional grammar, which, by itself, was a great feat. His constant chanting and remembrance of 'Rama Japa' seemed to have created such an aura around him that even the God of misfortune, Shanideva, could not touch him. In fact, it is believed in Indian mythology that Hanuman was the only one who did not come under the spell of Shanideva as he had such purity around him. Further, he was an embodiment of the practice of Brahmacharya.

Reflection Point

What is the value system that you profess dearly and would not trade them for anything?

Personal Observance of Yoga

Niyama, the second part of the eight-fold path of yoga, stands for observances that a person must carry out.

Shaucha, Santosha, Tapas, Svadhyaya and *Ishvara Pranidhana* are five categories of *Niyama.*

Shaucha

Shaucha stands for purification and cleanliness both of body and mind. An unclean environment and impurities of the mind can affect a person on the path of yoga, hindering spiritual advancement.

An impure mind means a restless mind. It also means an egoistic mind. Such a mind exploits others and does not contribute to others.

Santosha

Santosha is inner contentment. Acceptance is a very big part of this inner contentment. Acceptance of life and of what life has given you so that you learn to flow with experiences, rather than resisting them, helps create an environment of inner contentment. Learning to let go of pain and hurt is also important.

Tapas

Tapas or austerity is a strong yogic practice. *Tapas* actually means 'heat'. The heat or light energy you must generate to destroy inner darkness... heat to create order to destroy disorder in you. The *tapas* is, in fact, dropping of the 'past' that is interfering with the 'present' and thus allowing you to experience the richness of 'now' rather than getting lost in the greed for the 'future'.

When the 'will' is in harmony with life, it creates inner light - *tapas.* Meditation is a form of *tapas* that purifies the mind.

Svadhyaya

Svadhyaya is self-study. This is about understanding who you are through inner contemplation of the self. When you practice self-study, you realise you are not connected to the 'real' self but to the 'false' self. You relate to yourself and also, to others through a form of 'image'. You have an image of yourself and you also have an image of others. You have an illusion that the 'image' is the real self. The image can be a social construct or your expectations – that's the 'false' self. Observing all these is self-study or *svadhyaya.*

It is also about seeing the divinity within you and connecting with that divinity.

Ishvara Pranidhana

Ishvara Pranidhana means devotion, but it goes beyond that. It means surrendering of the 'false self' to a higher purpose by letting go of the ego. This is not just surrendering of the 'false self' getting lost to the greed of the 'future', but also surrendering of the fruits of your work to that higher purpose.

The classical example of such a character is seen from the epic, Mahabharata.

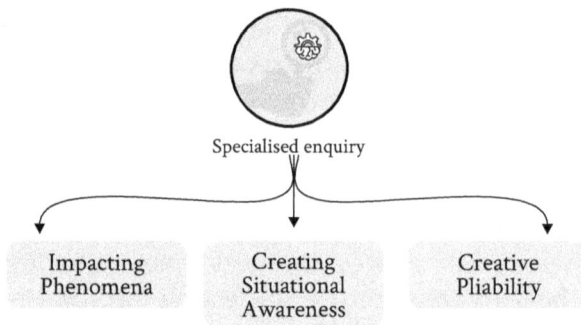

Impacting Phenomena	Creating Situational Awareness	Creative Pliability

Draupadi's father, Drupada conducted a sacrifice (a Yajna) in order to be blessed with a son. He wanted a son out of spite and vengeance. His son to be born (Dhrishtadyumna) was destined to kill Drupada's nemesis Drona. Draupadi was born out of that fire as Dhrishtadyumna's twin sister. Thus, Draupadi was born out of the fire of vengeance and passion. Yet, she was not wished for, by her father. She was a by-product of the Yajna (sacrifice).

She was desired in marriage, by many, for political gains. She was treated like an object to be distributed equally among the five brothers. She was humiliated after the game of dice; was almost abducted in the final year of exile. All her sons were murdered in their sleep which was against the norms of the war. Even after diligently performing all her duties towards her five husbands, Draupadi was criticised in the end by Yudhishthira for favouring Arjuna. Even after going through so much of agony, she displayed sanity and compassion in her life.

This is an ideal case of personal observance for a higher cause for which she was born and achieved that cause to perfection.

Reflection Point

Do you have in you the skill of 'personal observance' against all odds?

Learning Through Pigeon

Dattatreya was a noble child. As a child, his behaviour was notably restrained. He always kept his eyes and ears open, for he learned many things from nature. It is said he looked at life through 1000 eyes. In yogic paradigm, it's called *Sahasrara Chakra*... a lotus with 1000 petals.

Dattatreya observed a baby pigeon caught in a hunter's net. Its mother, in a state of utter panic, tried to free her baby and got caught in the net too. The father pigeon, seeing this and being attached to both mother and baby, tried to rescue them and was caught in the net.

When Dattatreya saw this, he said, "Look at the play of attachment!" The baby pigeon was beyond rescue, entangled as it was in the net, yet the attachment of the parents was so strong, that even without knowing how to help they tried to do something. The attachment of the parents entangled them further in the net.

As Lord Krishna says, by the sword of detachment, learn to cut asunder all your attachments. You must learn to practice detachment. Please note that detachment does not mean indifference. It means understanding the reality and inevitability of life.

Death is a part of that reality.

Reality of life is death. But the expectation of life is that you can't stand death. When you can't stand death, you fight with death. Death is a part and parcel of life. If you see it with a sense of detachment, you can use death to end the trauma of death. You cannot negotiate with death. Therefore, death is inevitable.

When death happens, can you negotiate with death? From there you learn how to bring death to end your yesterday. You must know how to bring death to your yesterday.

If you know how to do that, then you are alive to the today. Bring death to your expectation of today. When you do that, you live the poetry of today.

Death is worshipped in our country.

It may appear cruel to say this. It is extraordinary to see that death is a part and parcel of life. Your consciousness is attached to the body, like a mother to her child. When your consciousness is attached to the body, then the attachment to the body doesn't make you free from the limitations of the body. If your body is going through difficulty, can you keep your consciousness unattached to the body?

The body must die. See it. Death comes dancing to a wise person.

How is it applicable to both corporate and family life?

So often in the corporate world a person gets so attached to a position like CMD or CEO and thus in the process consciously or unconsciously does not groom his colleagues to grow, or, he establishes a gap between his position and those below him in hierarchy. Thus, his role makes him indispensable. How can an organisation grow under a person with such an attitude of attachment?

Is it not natural to be protective of one's position?

If you have a spiritual value of openness and trust in existence or in God, then nature will groom you for a better position which involves both yours as well as organisation's growth.

Reflect deeply on this story.

King Janaka was a disciple of the great sage and Master, Ashtavakra. The Master and his pupil had a special affinity for each other. They bonded so closely that the other disciples, who were sannyasins themselves, were envious of Janaka. They felt that Janaka undeservedly received a greater share of their Master's attention, as he was a wealthy and powerful King.

Janaka was once at a spiritual discourse by the sage, along with other disciples. The talk was on, while a messenger from Janaka's court, disrupted the assembly. The messenger reverentially bowed to the king and announced that a fire had broken out at the royal palace. A substantial part of Janaka's wealth was destroyed in the conflagration.

On hearing the messenger, Janaka ordered him to leave the assembly. Janaka was enraged that by not bowing to his Master, the messenger had disrespected him. Regarding the damages, Janaka declared that he did not worry about the losses. He regarded the knowledge that sage Ashtavakra gave him, was more valuable than all his material wealth.

A few days passed. Janaka continued to attend the spiritual discourses, disregarding the damages to his wealth.

In the middle of one such discourse, one of the hermitage's servants, rushed into the assembly. He announced that some monkeys had carried away all of the pupils' loincloths that they'd put out for drying. The pupils (sans Janaka) rushed out in panic, to the place where they had put out their loincloths for drying. On reaching the spot, however, they found that all their clothes were undisturbed. They remained where they'd left them originally. They returned to the hermitage, embarrassed.

On seeing them, the Master quipped, 'It should now be clear as to why Janaka is dear to me. All of you appear to have renounced this world. Nonetheless, you continue to be attached to something as trifling as the loincloths. Those loincloths, are worthless rag pieces for the rest of the world. You find them to be of greater value, however, than my discourses. On the other hand, Janaka was undisturbed by the fire to his palace and material wealth. The other day, he drove away his own messenger for disturbing this assembly. He has truly renounced everything; not the rest of you. He indeed is a true seeker; none of you.'

Reflection point

Is there a prayerful pause, prayerful shock and prayerful direction for you towards position, power and death?

Learning From a Python

If you look at a python, you will see that it is very lazy. It waits for its prey to come. Very rarely does it go and hunt. It prefers to wait. It has such tremendous patience to wait. And when something passes, it follows it and knows how to capitalise.

Dattatreya, looking at the python, learnt patience. People are so impatient! For most of you, foolishness is so deep, your impatience is so strong, and you become a patient of foolishness.

Being Patient

Don't be restless. In fact, if you are patient in life, you will know how to treat even your difficulties with respect. Patience gives you that kind of power.

By nature, a saint is so patient that he crowns his difficulties. Why? He doesn't worry about the tomorrow. Why? Because in his fist, he keeps the today. Treat difficulty with respect.

When you have patience, you will learn that the good times will follow, but they will follow only when they are meant to do so.

But why are you impatient? Have you ever thought about it? Because, your mind is always bent upon acquiring things. You want to acquire wealth, power, sexual pleasure, name, fame etc. Isn't the story of your life always centred on acquiring?

Reflect on this.

A Hindu saint was heading to the river Ganges to bathe. There was a family on its banks in commotion. The members were shouting at each other in anger.

He turned to his disciples, smiled and asked them, "When angry, why do we shout at each other?"

The disciples thought over it for a while and one of them responded, "We shout because we lose our calm."

"But, why should we shout when the other person is near us? We can as well tell him softly, whatever needs to be said, can't we?"

The disciples gave other answers too, but, none satisfied him.

Finally, the saint explained, "When two people are angry at each other, their hearts turn distant. They then shout, to cover that distance and be able to hear each other. The angrier they are, the stronger they need to shout."

He continued, "What happens when two people fall in love? They don't shout at each other, but, talk softly as their hearts are closer. The distance between them reduces..."

The saint further added, "How about when the love between them increases? They don't even need to speak. They whisper, get closer to each other. Ultimately, they needn't whisper too. They'd only have to look at each other and that'd be it. That's how close two people get, when fully in love."

He looked at his disciples and said, "So when you argue with someone, ensure your hearts don't drift apart. Don't utter words that'd push you away from each other. If not, there might come a day, when the distance between you would be so great that it'd make the return path long and weary."

Inspection Point

Is there a half-truth situation like this in your life... if so, which side are you looking at?

Learning From Earth

The great sage Dattatreya had many gurus. Possessing a mind not shackled by likes and dislikes, he was able to unravel many of the mysteries of life by observing them unfold before his eyes. The Earth was the first guru of Dattatreya and it taught him many valuable lessons.

He saw that on the Earth all things existed together and each of them had its own beauty. The river, the flora, the fauna, the mountains – all co-existed. The rose flower blooms and the cactus exists too, on the same Earth. One person is beautiful, another isn't, one is rich while another is poor. It is all the same consciousness, yet each one exists as per its *karma*. So, observing the Earth, Dattatreya realised the theory of *karma*. He realised too that if you can be at peace with your *karma*, then you are not in conflict with yourself.

You compare your *karma* with that of others and make your life miserable from this unnecessary comparison. When you can be at peace with your *karma*, you will see the beauty in all situations. A rose has its own beauty and so does a cactus. You all want to see things that are not in your fate and fail to see what is wonderful with your lot in life. This is the problem.

If you understand the theory of *karma*, then your mind takes on a different dimension. Don't search for your dreams in the sky, but look for truth on the earth, which is your dire need.

Dattatreya realised something else too when he contemplated further. He realised that the Earth gives so much but most of us are not thankful for it. Despite this ingratitude, it continues to do its duty. The Earth never stops giving.

If I look at most of you, you expect some thanks for the things you do. The Earth, however, gives out of love, without expecting anything in return.

Reflect on this story that I heard recently.

Once a king ordered his three ministers to take a bag, head to the forest and fill the bag with fruits.

The first minister thought that since the king had ordered for collection of fruits, he must collect the best of fruits in his bag.

The second minister thought that since the king was a very busy person, he would not look very thoroughly into the bag as to what has been collected and hence he collected whatever he could lay his hands on. Thus, his bag was filled up with a mixture of good as well as rotten fruits.

The third minister thought that the king might only see externally as to how big the bag was and thereby he just filled up his bag with dried leaves and dust.

All the three ministers returned to the court with their respective bags, having complied with the King's order for collecting fruits.

The King, without even seeing what their bags contained, just ordered that the three ministers be sent to separate jails for three weeks, where they would not be provided with any food and they were only allowed to carry their respective bags in which they had collected the fruits.

The first minister could spend the three weeks in the jail by eating all those good fruits he had collected.

The second one could survive for some time with the good fruits in the bag and later he developed ailments by eating the rotten fruits that he had collected.

The third minister had nothing to eat and hence could not survive.

From the above story, we'd understand that we must undergo the consequences of our own deeds.

"You will be suffering your own reactions as per your *karmas*. Every *karma* that you perform, you have to endure its consequences. Good and bad, everything, you must reap what you sow. No doubt about that.

In Mahabharata it is stated, "Amongst thousands of cows, a calf finds its own mother. Similarly, the results of your past *karma* (deeds) when fully ripe, will find you without fail."

Reflection Point

When will you employ your spiritual key in dealing with the results of your deeds or the effect of *karma*?

Learning From Air

Air (*Vayu*) was another guru of the great sage Dattatreya. If you observe the movement of air, for instance, you will realise that it has a certain quality – it touches and goes. Air can carry anything, but it is not polluted for long by what it carries. If you carry your disappointment or hurt in a similar way, and not allow them to become an intrinsic part of you, then the whole dimension of your life changes.

Touch an experience and allow that experience to go. If somebody has cheated you, you will naturally be disappointed, but you should not carry your disappointment with you for long. If you go through a divorce and must deal with the pain of divorce, experience the pain and let it go. You fail to do this. You hold on to the pain through memory and give life to dead things.

While dealing with people in life, you must have this touch and go approach. Learn to apply this in your life. Experience a sensation and let it go.

Reflect on your disappointment or hurt, in the corporate or in the family world. Do not identify with them but allow them to be part of you.

I recall a nice story that I heard.

A monk decided to meditate alone, away from his monastery. He took his boat out to the middle of the lake, moored it there, closed his eyes and began meditation.

After a few hours of undisturbed silence, he suddenly felt the bump of another boat colliding with his own. With his eyes still closed, he sensed his anger rising, and by the time he opened his eyes, he was ready to scream at the boatman who dared to disturb him in his meditation.

But when he opened his eyes, he saw that it was an empty boat that had probably got untethered and floated to the middle of the lake.

At that moment, the monk achieved self-realisation, and understood that anger was within him; it merely needed the bump of an external object to be provoked in him.

From then on, whenever he came across someone who irritated him or provoked him to anger, he reminded himself, "The other person is merely an empty boat. The anger is within me."

Reflection Point

Can you identify your real life conflicting relationship scenario where you have applied the principle of 'Touch and Go'?

Learning From the Sun

Another guru of the sage Dattatreya was the Sun. There is an external Sun and an internal Sun. The *Gayathri Mantra,* for example, unfolds not just of the external Sun, but the internal one also. The Sun lights up everything from the gutters of a city to its gardens, but sunlight is not affected by anything on which it falls. It is not contaminated.

Look inside you. There is sunlight, a certain consciousness, inside all of you. It lights up everything from the gutters of your minds to the benedictions of your love. Yet, this consciousness, this sunlight, is neither affected by your thoughts nor your emotions. You should discover this sunlight. Unless you do, you will be crushed by the situations of life.

Meditation is about closing your eyes and seeing that light. If you can discover that consciousness, then that is meditation.

Hence, the Sun is a great teacher.

Learning From Fire, Water and Space

Agni (fire) can burn you. It can also give you warmth. If you come too close to it, you will get burnt and if you are too far then you will not feel its warmth. This is true of life too. In any situation, try not to be too attached or too detached. Learn to put everything in its appropriate place. Fire burns both garbage and diamond without differentiation. So too in life, one should be objective in orientation.

Water teaches you flexibility. Just see how a river is committed to reaching the ocean. As it flows through valleys and mountains, it bonds with the terrain. Similarly, you should learn to blend with the situations in life. Be flexible. Adapt. Are you flexible? For example, a river, whatever be the obstacle in its path, flows flexibly around it; it flows under and over the mountains. If there is resistance in its way, it flows around the obstacle and finds a way to reach the ocean.

Aakasha is the Sanskrit word for space. *Aakasha* can be contained in a room and outside it too. If you observe space, you can learn a lot from it. There is space in the room called room space. When the room is destroyed, the room space is destroyed too, but, not space itself *per se*. In fact, the room is in space – space is not limited by the room.

So too, consciousness is in the body. When the body is destroyed consciousness appears to be destroyed. The body is in consciousness and consciousness is not limited by the body. So, like space, consciousness too is unlimited. If you can operate from unlimited consciousness, then there are unlimited possibilities in life.

A farmer lost a clock that was of great sentimental value and he searched everywhere in a room to try and find it, calling all his friends to help him look for it. A young boy came and asked if he could try his luck at finding the clock. The boy meditated alone in the room and, after a few moments of silence, found the clock. The farmer asked the boy how he managed to find it when all others had failed. The boy replied that after everyone was gone and he sat in silence, he was able to hear the ticking of the clock and hence locate it. When everyone was searching for it, there was noise and thereby the clock's ticks could not be heard.

If you can silence yourself, and come from that space, you will understand something very different. If God has created life, then there must be some pattern in the problems of life. If you give space, there is silence and in that silent space, there is a different knowing.

Reflection Point

Will you see through special eyes the qualities of fire, water and space in your mundane activities and learn from them?

Churning of the Ocean

The story goes that the *Devas* (demi-gods) were slowly losing their strength because of a curse by a great *rishi*. Their arch rivals the *Asuras* (demons) took advantage of this opportunity and threatened to wage a war against the *Devas*. Fearful of what may come to pass, the demi-gods approached Lord Vishnu (known as the Preserver in the Trinity of Hinduism) for a solution. The great Lord told them to churn the primordial 'Ocean of Milk' or *Ksheera Sagara* to receive *Amrita*, the nectar of immortality, through which they may regain, their strength.

This churning, however, was not so easy a task that it could be conducted by the demi-gods by themselves. So they forged a temporary peace with the demons to reach their goal, after which the nectar was to be distributed equally between the demons and the demi-gods. Using the King of Serpents as the churning rope and Mount Mandara as the churning stick, the demi-gods and demons began a task that would take 1000 years to complete. Lord Vishnu, incarnated as *Kurma* i.e., as a tortoise and held Mount Mandara on His back to prevent it from sinking into the ocean during the churning.

They worked tirelessly for centuries; the reward they sought was not easy to attain. The first thing to come out was not the nectar, but poison. The *Halahalam*, as it was called, was so potent that it enveloped the universe and threatened to destroy all. Lord Shiva (known as the Destroyer in the Trinity of Hinduism) stepped forward to take this poison. His wife, Goddess Parvathi, prevented it from spreading to the whole body by restraining it to His throat. Lord Shiva's name Neelakanta or 'blue-throated one' is derived from this incident; the poison having turned His neck blue, due to its potency.

Amrita, the nectar of immortality, was almost the last thing to come out of the ocean. When it did, it was held in a *kumbh* (pot) by Dhanvantari, the physician of the *devas*. Fearful of the consequences of what might transpire, the demi-gods persuaded the demons out of drinking from the pot. Lord Vishnu incarnated again in the form of Mohini, the irresistible temptress, and persuaded the demons to hand over the pot to her. What ensued was a dozen days and nights of fighting between the two groups.

During this time, as Lord Vishnu fled with the nectar pot from earth to heaven, a few drops of the nectar fell on four places in India: Haridwar, Prayag (Allahabad), Nashik and Ujjain. It is in these places that the *Kumbh Mela*, one of the largest religious festivals in the world, takes place on a rotational basis, every 3 years. By the time it has rotated to the other three sites and returned to one of the places, 12 years (representing 12 days and nights of fighting) will have passed by. Millions upon millions of devotees would have paid homage at the holy site. Even today, bathing in the rivers of Ganga, Yamuna, Godavari and Shipra, where the nectar drops fell, is considered sacred and is believed, that it washes away sins.

Learning From the Churning

Watching the ocean of humanity that churns in and out of the sacred place is not unlike the ocean's churning in the story. In fact, it is like the turmoil that takes place continually inside many of you.

The mind is constantly being churned by the positive (represented by demi-gods) and negative (represented by demons) aspects within you. For the spiritual seeker, one part will yearn to pursue the spiritual path, another will oppose it. Both these aspects must be in harmony. Keep in mind that both the *Devas* and the *Asuras* worked together for the churning. This painful churning brings out first suffering and unhappiness before it gives any rewards. It is the *Halahalam* that threatens to destroy. Lord Shiva, who drinks that poison, represents the ascetic principle. He represents simplicity, pure love, discipline, courage and detachment. The poisonous instability of your minds can only be stopped by cultivating these principles within you.

Devas and *asuras* are brothers. Symbolically meaning that both good and bad are in you, hence these are like brothers too. The ocean represents life. The churning of the ocean represents the constant churn between the good and the bad in you. *Devas are* led by the good while *asuras* by the bad; both vibes are in you. While the churning happens, the poison comes out...the toxin in you comes out.

When toxicity is thrown out, it affects people around you. Hence Lord Shiva, the symbol of ultimate energy takes in the poison and Goddess Parvati stops it at the region of the throat – meaning the toxin should not destroy one who takes it or throws it out to cause damage. That subtle positioning is the spiritual acumen. For example, a student's toxicity is thrown out through spiritual practice. The Guru must take in that toxicity and not allow it to spread out.

While absorbing the toxins, the Guru should not be destroyed. On the other hand, by not absorbing the toxins, the others will be destroyed. That subtle positioning is represented by Lord Shiva (Neelakanta).

The Serpent King represents desire. Mount Mandara stands for concentration. The name 'Mandara' contains two words: *'man'* meaning 'the mind' and *'dara'* meaning 'straight-line'. Therefore the name itself stands for the concentration of the mind. The mind, like Mount Mandara during the churning, must rest itself upon divinity (Lord Vishnu's incarnation as the tortoise) and give itself up to that divinity, if it should not sink into the ocean.

The divinity of the tortoise stands for discipline and flexibility. When required, it withdraws into its shell. The shell represents strength. Strength should not be crushed by the circumstances of life.

Therefore, desire must be held in firm hands and controlled, the mind focused on a single aim, rested upon divinity, with all your negative and positive aspects harmonised if spiritual enlightenment is to be attained. What keeps you from this enlightenment and the immortality that it represents?

> "
>
> Lord Vishnu in the form of Mohini represents the delusion of the mind. It is the delusion of pride and ego. They are the last hurdles that you have to overcome. "

Amrita represents ultimate enlightenment or *Moksha*. How is this relevant in a corporate or in the family context?

The ocean represents life. Both poison and nectar are part of life. In each one's life, doesn't poison and nectar exist? Isn't there a snake, in the form of desire that is constantly churning?

In the family or corporate setup, aren't both good and bad operating? In all inter-relationships of life, the toxins are represented by anger, hurt, jealousy etc., When churned, all these surface, be it in family or in the corporate set-up.

A leader will have to absorb toxins, whenever they are released. Else, the very fabric of family or corporate setup would be destroyed. But the leader is not destroyed in the process. Hence, like Lord Shiva, he must position negative energy in such a way that it does not destroy him or his family or his team.

Mandara represents focus and concentration on which, desire i.e., the snake, must be centred and managed. The corporate setup should be focused, the family should have focus too. The focus anchored on the tortoise indicates seating the discipline of withdrawal when required and not crushed by circumstances, i.e., protected by the tortoise shell.

The ultimate result is *amrita*, nectar which is profitable growth, in a corporate or family setting. This profitable growth results in inner freedom.

An organisation or family without ultimate freedom is nothing but the movement of bondage symbolising struggle.

The *amrita* that falls in four places means cosmic divine energy exists in those fields. In life too, there are fields of positivity and negativity. The field of positivity must be worshipped, hence the *Kumbh*.

Spiritual seekers gather at *Kumbh Mela* to bathe in the rivers there. They want to wash away their sins. The festival is called the *Kumbh Mela*, one of the largest peaceful gatherings in the world.

Reflection Point

Can you employ your spiritual key to learn from the churning in your life?

The Symbolism of Gods From Indian Culture for Life Management

From the earliest days of creation, especially after the ocean churning, when the demons were deceived by Lord Vishnu's strategy, gods and demons have been waging a bitter and continuous war for the domination of the worlds. Demons occasionally gain overwhelming strength, threaten Indra's powers, and peace in the world. Whenever they gain ascendancy, gods seek the help of the Trinity, to defeat them and thereby protect the heavens as well as their powers.

Symbolically, gods represent the pleasure principle and the demons the pain principle. Since both these qualities impact our bodies, we are subject to pain and pleasure. Since these qualities reside in the human body, it is considered the field of Nature (*kshetra*). Depending upon who has the superior strength in our bodies, we may experience pain or pleasure, knowledge or ignorance, right thinking or delusion.

The food we consume can become an offering to either godly nature or demonic nature as both resides in us. Although all organs of the body are considered divinities, they are susceptible to evil desires and intentions. Only breath is unaffected by it. Hence, it is important that we practice self-restraint, cultivate purity, and offer food to gods before we eat so that only godly nature in the body is nourished by it, and not the demonic nature.

Godly nature in us gains strength when the body is predominated by *sattva* and the mind is filled with divine thoughts. The scriptures suggest that to abide by good conduct, human beings should eat *sattvic* food, offer the food to gods before eating it, perform daily and periodic sacrifices, abide by *dharma*, virtuous conduct and practice devotion.

If the demonic nature gains strength, the body becomes a virtual hell, with the darkness and grossness of *rajas* and *tamas*, pride, egoism, envy, delusion and other impurities. Hence, to protect ourselves from the demonic influences, it is necessary for us to cultivate virtue, practice *dharma*, acquire the right knowledge and work for liberation.

The worship of gods and chanting of mantras, thus assumes great significance, in our existence.

Uddhava and Lord Krishna – a Dialogue

Uddhava was Lord Krishna's cousin and a close friend, like Arjuna. Uddhava was among the first Yadavas to befriend Krishna, as a child. They remained friends from their childhood.

Lord Krishna was preparing to return to Vaikunta, His abode, as the 8th incarnation was complete. He granted a boon to Uddhava for all the services rendered to Him.

Uddhava had never sought anything for himself, all along, though he had moved closely with Lord Krishna. He did not desire any materialistic wealth or comforts. He was, however, curious about the way Lord Krishna had decided to act in certain critical situations. Uddhava felt that Lord Krishna's preaching and practices were not in sync, at certain times. Lord Krishna consented to discuss. The dialogue that ensued is known as 'Uddhava Gita.'

Uddhava: Krishna, first tell me who's a true friend?

Lord Krishna: One who helps another in need, is a true friend.

Uddhava: Krishna, you are a dear friend of the Pandavas. They trust you fully as an 'Apat bandhava' (one who protects in distress). You are a great gyani. You know everything – from the past, present and the future. Why didn't you act like a true friend when they needed you the most? Why didn't you prevent Dharmaraja's (Yudhishthira) participation in the game of dice? You may have had valid reasons for that. Even if so, why didn't you turn Dharmaraja's luck in his favour? Wouldn't that have ensured the prevalence of dharma?

You could even have stopped the game after Dharmaraja lost his wealth, country and himself. Doing that may have saved Dharmaraja from being punished for gambling.

Or still, you could have entered the hall when he started betting on his brothers. Your inaction in a way prompted Duryodhana to lure

Dharmaraja to the next step. He offered to return everything that he'd lost if he'd bet on Draupadi (she who always brought good fortune to the Pandavas). You were conspicuously absent at this point too.

You did intervene though, in the eleventh hour. That only happened on the verge of Draupadi's disrobing. She ran the risk of being put to great disrespect and shame. You enrobed her and saved her from further humiliation. I know you'll say you protected her by doing this. How would you justify that you protected or saved a woman subjected to such shaming when she was dragged mercilessly in front of so many men in that hall? Who or what did you save, by acting thus?

Is it fair to call you 'Apat bandhava'? Is this Dharma?

Uddhava's posers brought tears to his own eyes.

Lord Krishna smiled all the while, and He responded.

"Dear Uddhava, let me recount a universal principle, that'd answer your questions: 'It's one's 'Viveka' (prudence) that wins. Duryodhana had viveka, Dharmaraja did not. Consequently, Dharmaraja lost.

Duryodhana had sufficient resources – money and wealth - to gamble with, but, he did not know how to play the game of dice. He cleverly requested his uncle Shakuni to play the game, while he placed the bets. That's viveka. Dharmaraja could have used viveka too and requested me to play the game, on his behalf. Had that happened, tell Me who'd have won? Could Shakuni have rolled out the numbers I'd have called or would I have done the rolling at his calls, better?

Ok, let's move on. Dharmaraja may not have deemed it fit to include me in the game. But, further on too, Dharmaraja exhibited his lack of viveka. He prayed that I should not come into that hall. He did not want Me to know that he was ill-fated and as such, compelled to play that game. His prayers bound me and prevented my coming to the hall. I was always around to help. I waited that someone might pray and call me in. When the losses of Bheema, Arjuna, Nakula and Sahadeva happened, they just cursed Duryodhana and lamented about their fates. It never occurred to them to seek My help.

Draupadi too did not call out to Me when Dushyasana dragged her by her hair. Dushyasana did that to comply with his brother's orders. Draupadi chose to argue in that hall, as per her capability. But, she never sought for Me.

It was then that good sense prevailed when Dushyasana started disrobing her. She screamed, 'Hari, Hari, Abhayam Krishna, Abhayam,' – calling out to Me.

That's when I got the opportunity to save her modesty. The moment she called, I stepped in. I saved her modesty. What's my fault in all of this?"

Uddhava: Wonderful explanation, Krishna. I'm impressed. But, may I ask you another question?

Lord Krishna nodded in affirmation.

Uddhava: Would it imply that you'll come in only when asked. Will you not come on your own to help people in crisis, to establish justice?

Lord Krishna (smiles): Uddhava, everyone's life proceeds as per their karmas. I don't run it for them. I don't interfere with it. I am merely a 'witness'. I stand near them and observe whatever is happening. That's My Dharma.

Uddhava: That's amazing Krishna. If so, you'll stand close to us, observe all our evil deeds and, as we continue to commit further sins, you'll keep a watch on us. You want us to commit more blunders, accumulate sins and suffer!

Lord Krishna: Uddhava, try to realise the deeper meaning of what you just stated. If you realise that I witness whatever you do, would you do anything wrong or bad? You constantly forget this and think that you can do things without my knowledge. That's when you get into trouble. Dharmaraja's ignorance was in thinking that he could play the game of dice, without my knowing it. If Dharmaraja had remembered that I was present at all times around everyone, as 'Sakshi' (witness), wouldn't the game have finished differently?

Uddhava: What profound philosophy, Keshava. What a great truth! Even while praying or, performing poojas seeking His help, we feel that these are nothing but our feelings and beliefs. When we start believing that nothing moves without the Lord's grace, how can we not feel His presence as 'Sakshi'? How can we forget this and act?

Throughout Bhagavad Gita, this was the very philosophy that Lord Krishna imparted to Arjuna. He was Arjuna's charioteer as well friend, philosopher and guide, but He did not fight Arjuna's War.

Realise that the Ultimate *Sakshi* or the one who is the Witness... is within you! Discover that God Consciousness! Discover thy higher self – the pure loveful and blissful Supreme One. Please realise that God is within you at all times – when you do good things, as well as when you commit mistakes. If you seek His help to play your games of dice in life, he will win it for you. If instead, you play it yourselves, by yourself and for yourself, you'll not receive His help and also, lose as Dharmaraja did, everything in life!

Reflection Point

Can you bring in this understanding where everything happens through the grace of the Lord while you move into the significance of gods and their worship that you offer?

With this understanding, I invite you to read further on the significance of various gods and goddesses that we worship! These unfold life-nourishing recipes for spiritual living.

Lord Ganesha

The wise sages of India chose symbols to represent timeless truths. Time does not distort symbols as easily as it does with words, and many truths of wise men are contained today in the symbolic idols we worship. The representation of Lord Ganesha is no different.

During the festival of Ganesh Chaturthi, we see many idols of the Lord displayed in homes and communities, garlanded with love and devotion.

Ganesha will beam a silent message to all of us, as He has done from time immemorial.

Are we listening? Let us learn what He can teach us.

His Attributes

The Ganapathi Upanishad of *Rishi Atharva* expounds on the different attributes of Ganesha – He is the son of Lord Shiva, the God of destruction and Goddess Parvati. He is revered as the remover of obstacles, the Lord of success and the patron of arts, sciences and travelling.

He is also defined as *Omkara*, 'having the form of *Om*', the first sound after Energy (*Shakti*) and Matter (Shiva) meet. We invoke Him before the start of any auspicious activity for its unhindered performance.

Ganesha symbolises the equilibrium between power and beauty, force and kindness. His name itself reveals His qualities.

gana means 'hosts, group, collection, or categories'. It can also be armies, any large number of things or people.

isha means 'master'.

gana+isha is 'master of hosts'.

The Elephant Head

This, the most distinguishing feature of Ganesha, denotes intelligence, discriminative powers.

The *trishula* mark on his hand (trident - the weapon of Lord Shiva), indicates his lordship over time.

His large ears show an ability to listen to people who seek help. They denote wisdom and highlight the importance of listening to gain knowledge.

There is only one tusk on Ganesha's head, the other one being cut off or broken. This singular tusk shows his ability to 'breakthrough' all forms of dualism. There are, however, other meanings associated with this single tusk.

The curved trunk of Ganesha shows the intellectual potential that gives him the faculty to discriminate between the real and the unreal. The curved trunk can pick up a needle or pull out a tree, thus symbolising deftness and strength.

The Belly
It is said to contain infinite universes and signifies his capacity to swallow the sorrows of the Universe and protect the world. It represents the capacity to digest all.

Vasuki, the serpent king, wrapped around Ganesha's belly represents the divine energy, in all its forms, pervading all living beings. It also denotes that the snake, when uncoiled, represents the maximising of one's potential, the *Kundalini Shakti* within.

The Legs
One leg is always resting on the ground and the other is raised. The legs remind us that we must participate in the material world as well as in the spiritual world. We must learn to live in the world, without being worldly.

The Arms
Each of His four arms represents the subtle body of a man: mind, intellect, ego and conditioned conscience. They too symbolise something beautiful.

Axe – the Lord strikes at obstacles and cuts off all attachment through devotion.

Whip – to those with devotion, the whip symbolically pulls devotees through love. This is to tie us to the beauty of God; we must learn to be free from worldly desires. He is more commonly seen with a bowl of sweets in this hand - they are rewards given out for penances performed.

A pose of blessing – the third hand of Ganesha has the palm open outward - it is always showering us with love and blessings.

Lotus – this represents the inner realised self.

Lord Brahma, the Creator

Lord Brahma's icon has four heads (*chaturmukha brahma*) facing the four directions. They represent the four *Vedas* (*Rik, Yajur, Sama, Atharvana*). Vedas are the insights emerging out of egoless state of consciousness. The *four yugas* or epochs (*Krita, Treta, Dwapara, Kali*) represent infinity of time which goes into cyclic formation. The four *varnas* or classification of labour in a society (*Brahmana, Kshatriya, Vaisya, Sudra*) represent the four forms of energy needed for any family or nation's well-being without one feeling high or low about the energy field. The four faces are represented in meditation.

There are four arms holding up different objects, *Akshamala* (rosary), *Kurcha* (kusha grass), *Sruk* (ladle), *Sruva* (spoon), *Kamandala* (water pot) and *Pustaka* (book) and in different poses representing the four directions. Their combination and arrangement, vary with the image.

Akshamala symbolises the process of purifying the mind through *japa* or meditation; *kamandala* represents simple life. The implements *kusha, sruk* and *sruva*, denote the system of sacrifices for invoking the divine, which is beyond ordinary comprehension. The book represents the wisdom of life. Hand postures (*mudras*) are *abhaya* (protector) and *varada* (giver of boons). The icon may be in standing posture on a lotus or in sitting posture on a *hamsa* (swan). *Hamsa* stands for wisdom and discrimination.

Lord Brahma stands for creativity. In each aspect of your life, can there be a new energy of creativity, in routine activities? This is the energy of Lord Brahma or creativity that you must strive for.

Lord Vishnu, the Sustainer

Lord Vishnu is also known as Mahavishnu, the great sustainer. Lord Vishnu means the one who pervades. Another name which is common is *Narayana*. Lord Vishnu is worshipped directly or in the *avatar* form of Lord Rama and Lord Krishna.

In one hand, he holds a conch. The conch represents the call of the Lord through our difficulties or good fortunes. The call awakens us to walk the path of goodness so that we are not pulled aside by evil or ego. In another hand, he holds a disc. If the call is not respected, then one will be punished appropriately. In the third hand, he holds a mace. The mace represents the constant knock for one to transform from the unconsciousness state to a consciousness state, through difficulties. In the fourth, he holds a lotus. Lotus symbolises that we can live unaffected by the world.

From his navel emerges Lord Brahma, representing that creativity should emerge from the core of ones' being. Lord Vishnu reclines on a serpent with thousand heads meaning that with infinite time he is resting. One must relax in time. Generally, one is always busy and tense with time. One conflicts with time and not in peace with it. Lord Vishnu rests in peace with time. The milky ocean represents purity. You should live in purity, live in peace but most often people live in greed, live in pleasure.

To be a devotee of Lord Vishnu, you must live and float in purity, rest relaxingly. It is only then that Goddess Lakshmi, the goddess of wealth, would patronise you and Lord Brahma – creativity will emerge in you.

The mantra for invocation is – *"Om Vishnave Namah or Om Narayanaya Namah"*.

The art of bringing Lord Vishnu's energy in life is through the power to sustain your creativity which Lord Vishnu represents. This creativity must be brought into your daily activities of life, with purity in it.

Hence, in organisations, there is a great deal of emphasis on sustainability.

Lord Shiva, the Destroyer

Lord Shiva symbolises death. Shiva also means auspiciousness, *mangalam*.

Death is not an end of life but a part of it. The art of wise dying is a part of wise living. Shiva means auspicious. Death is very auspicious, and the death of ignorance is the most auspicious. *Shivarathri* means bringing the light of auspiciousness to the realm of *rathri*, night or to bring the light of wisdom to the darkness in an individual.

On his head is river Ganges – the flow of wisdom. He has a moon which reflects a calm mind. When wisdom is present, mind is calm. On his neck, there is a snake. Snake stands for desire. But desire or the snake does not harm him meaning the desire is not harming the wise person. For an ordinary person, desire creates hell but to the wise the desire is indeed ornamentation. In other words, he is the master of desires. Lord Shiva has a third eye – the eye of intuition. When the mind is calm, wisdom flows and desire does not harm. In such a state the eye of intuition opens.

He is seated on deer-skin indicating that he is in austerity. Greatest austerity is the death of the ego. In one of his hands, he has a *trishula* – a trident – reflecting that he is the master of the three *gunas* or attributes – *sattwa, rajo* and *thamo guna*. He has a rosary – *japa mala* depicting his mind is in incantation always. He has a *kamandala* – a bowl representing his living a simple life. Living a simple life is better than living a complicated life. When you worship Lord Shiva with devotion and understanding, you destroy your ignorance and sorrow.

The mantra for invocation is – *"Om Namah Shivaya."*

Bhagaritha was a renowned king and forefather of Lord Rama of Raghu dynasty.

His forefathers known as Sagaras were burnt down due to a curse. For the upliftment of those ancestors from the cursed state to get to the heavens, he wanted to bring the river Ganga to earth. The idea was that when Ganga waters touched the ash of Sagaras, they would be absolved of their sins. He performed very severe austerities and got the permission from Indra.

He was permitted to bring Ganga which flowed in heaven, to the earth; however, he added that descending to the earth would be Ganga's decision. So Bhagaritha again started his penance and prayed to goddess Ganga. She agreed to descend, but warned him that he should find a person who could withstand the force with which she will descend to earth! He agreed and found out that the refuge would be with Lord Shiva. He performed austerities to please Lord Shiva.

Appreciating his devotion and efforts, Lord Shiva agreed to hold Ganga when she descends to the earth. Ganga out of her pride and ignorance thought that the Lord won't be able to withstand the force! She came down with an intention to gush down the Lord with heavy force.

Can the Lord, who holds the entire world He created, be pushed down by a River? The Lord, who is the creator of the entire universe and who has taken the forms just to shower His grace on creatures, arrested her flow in His matted hair! She tried her best to rush out of His matted hair but in vain. Not a drop of water could escape! Bhagaritha, worried by this (as he would not get Ganga to the earth otherwise), prayed to the Lord to show mercy on her.

The Gracious Lord allowed Ganga through a strand of His matted hair. Ganga then flowed humbly, gracefully and giving prosperity on her way to her destination. Thus, the ancestors of Bhagaritha were resurrected by the holy water of Ganga.

The Lord in the posture holding the Ganga in the matted hair is called Gangadhara Murthy.

Bhagiratha's bringing down the waters of Ganga to the earth, from the heavens, indicates *Bhagiratha Prayatna* or his stupendous effort in bringing a heavenly solution to the earth... a solution from the heaven to earth means making impossible as possible.

In life too, one should put in the efforts of Bhagiratha, turning the impossible to possible.

Bringing the energy of Lord Shiva in life is akin to learning the art of relegating death to the past and being alive, in the present. Most of us are a continuation of the past, hence our present is an extension of the past. Lord Shiva's energy represents the art of dying being confined to yesterday and, the awareness of being alive today.

Goddess Saraswati

Saraswati is a Sanskrit compound word of *sāra* which means "essence", and *sva* which means "oneself", the entire word meaning "essence of oneself" and Saraswati meaning "one who bestows the essence of self-knowledge".

Saraswati, the goddess of knowledge and arts, represents the free flow of wisdom and consciousness. She is the mother of the Vedas, and chants directed to her, called the *'Saraswativandana'* often begin and end Vedic lessons.

She is the epitome of perfect learning, which culminates in the detachment from material opulence. It is believed that goddess Saraswati endows human beings with the powers of speech, wisdom and learning. She has four hands representing four aspects of human personality in learning: mind, intellect, alertness and ego.

In visual representations, she has sacred scriptures in one hand and a lotus – the symbol of true knowledge – in the opposite hand.

With her other two hands, Saraswati plays the music of love and life on a string instrument called the *veena*. She is dressed in white – the symbol of purity – and rides on a white swan, symbolising *Sattwa Guna* (purity and discrimination). Her swan is a mythical bird, which, when offered a mixture of milk and water, is able to drink the milk, leaving the water behind, from the mixture. The *nyaya (logic)* is called *'Hamsa-ksheera-nyaya'* in the Vedic system, and is used as a maxim for one's discriminating ability.

Saraswati is also a prominent figure in Buddhist iconography too – the consort of Manjushri.

Learned and the erudite individuals attach great importance to the worship of goddess Saraswati as a representation of knowledge and wisdom. They believe that only Saraswati can grant them *moksha* – the final liberation of the soul.

Goddess Lakshmi

Goddess Lakshmi symbolises good luck. The word *Lakshmi* is derived from the Sanskrit word *Lakshya*, meaning "aim" or "goal," and in the Hindu faith, she is the goddess of wealth and prosperity of all forms, both material and spiritual.

For most Hindu families, Goddess Lakshmi is the household goddess, and she is a particular favourite among women. Although she is worshipped daily, the festive month of October is Goddess Lakshmi's special month.

Lakshmi Puja is celebrated on the full moon night of Kojagari Purnima, the harvest festival that marks the end of the monsoon season.

Goddess Lakshmi is the wife of Lord Vishnu, whom she accompanied, taking different forms in each of his incarnations.

Goddess Lakshmi is usually depicted as a beautiful woman of golden complexion, with four hands, sitting or standing on a full-bloomed lotus and holding a lotus bud, which stands for beauty, purity, and fertility. Her four hands represent the four ends of human life: *dharma* or righteousness, *kama* or desires, *Artha* or wealth, and *moksha* or liberation from the cycle of birth and death.

Cascading gold coins are often seen flowing from her hands, suggesting that those who worship her will gain wealth. She always wears gold embroidered red clothes. Red symbolises activity, and the golden lining indicates prosperity.

Goddess Lakshmi symbolises the active energy of Vishnu. Goddess Lakshmi and Lord Vishnu often appear together as *Lakshmi-Narayana* — Goddess Lakshmi accompanying Lord Vishnu.

Two elephants are often shown standing next to the goddess and spraying water. This denotes that ceaseless effort, when practised in accordance with one's *dharma* and governed by wisdom and purity, leads to both material and spiritual prosperity.

To symbolise her many attributes, Goddess Lakshmi may appear in any of her eight different forms, representing everything from knowledge to food grains.

Goddess symbolises not just material wealth but the wealth of all kinds of food to fame. Hence, she has many aspects representing various forms of wealth. Hindu tradition recognises eight forms of Goddess Lakshmi collectively known as *Ashtalakshmis* (eight Lakshmis), each representing a particular type of wealth, namely: *Adilakshmi* (primal), *Dhanyalakshmi* (crops), *Dhairyalakshmi* (courage), *Gajalakshmi* (elephants), *Santanalakshmi* (children), *Vijayalakshmi* (victory), *Vidyalakshmi* (education), and *Dhanalakshmi* (riches). Of these *Gajalakshmi* is the most popular, most likely because elephants were considered a great source of strength and victory on the battlefield, for kings, in the ancient times. There are some variations to the following list, but we consider this to be the standard based on the prayer, *Ashta Lakshmi Stotram*.

The importance attached to the presence of Goddess Lakshmi in every household makes her an essentially domestic deity. Householders worship Goddess Lakshmi as a symbol providing for the well-being and prosperity of the family. Fridays are traditionally the day on which Goddess Lakshmi is worshipped. Entrepreneurs also celebrate her as a symbol of prosperity and offer her daily prayers.

Annual Worship of Goddess Lakshmi

On the full moon night following Dusshera or Durga Puja, Hindus worship Goddess Lakshmi ceremonially at home, pray for her blessings.

It is believed that on this full moon night the goddess herself visits the homes and bestows the inhabitants with wealth. A special worship is also offered to Goddess Lakshmi on the auspicious Diwali night, the festival of lights.

Goddess Durga

Ramba was an *Asura* chieftain, who fell in love with a princess called Yamini, who was living a cursed existence as a buffalo. They married and the child born out of this union was named *Mahisha*, meaning buffalo... representing foolishness.

Mahishaasura, the buffalo demon, was a mighty tyrant. He had inherited the power of enchantment from his *Asura* father and the form of a buffalo from his mother. He could, however, change form at will and he terrorised the earth, empowered by his brute strength and enchantment. All inhabitants of the earth feared him. His ambition was to gain lordship over the three realms of heaven, earth and the nether-world. Being the son of an *asura* chieftain, the netherworld was his birth right. However, the other two spheres of existence needed to be conquered and for that, he needed more than just muscle power.

Following the advice of his elders, *Mahisha* proceeded to perform a penance, to please the Creator seeking the boon of immortality. He practised severe austerities, meditating on Lord Brahma. He consumed neither food nor water, and stood on one leg, focusing on nothing but the Creator. In due course, ant hills formed over his massive body, vines crept over it and a mound covered the *Asura* completely. His austerities were so powerful that flames emanated from his being, with a foul smoke accompanying it. The entire creation suffocated from these fumes and even heavens swayed to the power of his penance.

Indra, king of the gods, was perturbed. *Mahisha* was a tyrant and his penance only meant doom, for he was sure to seek boons from the Creator that would endanger world peace. He, therefore, ordered Vaayu, Varuna and Agni to disturb the efforts of the *Asura* by using their celestial powers. They readily obeyed. Vaayu created gales and storms over *Mahisha's* penance spot and when they did nothing, he channelled the winds to form cyclones. None of these affected *Mahisha's* penance. Varuna and Agni too could do nothing as their floods and fireballs went in vain. The three of them together were also of not much effect for so focused was *Mahishaasura*. Indra himself stepped in. Being the rain-god, he showered *Mahisha* with the fiercest thunderstorms. The *Asura's* intense meditation was still unaffected.

Ultimately, the Creator Lord Brahma had to descend to the earth on his swan-driven chariot. With one drop of the holy water of Ganga from his *kamandala*, he cleansed *Mahisha's* body of all that had grown over it. The flames were doused, and fresh air flowed over the earth.

"I have come, *Mahisha*, son of Ramba. I am pleased with your penance and have come to grant you your wishes. Ask Me what you wish for," said Lord Brahma.

"O Creator, if my efforts have truly pleased you, then reward me by granting me the coveted boon of immortality. Let me never face death. Let my body endure every force in the world and survive unto eternity," said the *Asura*. Lord Brahma expected him to ask exactly this. However, immortality was something he could not grant anyone. During Creation, he had decreed an end to everybody and everything and it was not in his power to disturb the balance of Creation by conferring immortality on anything that had a predestined end. He explained this to *Mahisha*.

"*Mahisha*, how do you expect me to grant you immortality? Ask me something else, child."

Mahisha was somewhat disappointed. He was unwilling to accept defeat though. He thought of how best he could work around Brahma's constraints and obtain for himself something that was the equivalent of immortality. Then, he spoke. "Brahmadeva, if such be Your constraint that you cannot grant me immortality, then let death come to me only at the hands of a woman. Let no other form of creation be capable of slaying me." Lord Brahma smiled at him. "So be it," said he, and disappeared.

Mahisha laughed out loud. He thought himself victorious. Being an *Asura*, one possessed of great physical strength and very little by way of intellectual proficiency, he was a chauvinist who believed that men were stronger than women. He believed that immunity from death at the hands of men, *devas* and others, i.e., those capable of slaying him, was as good as immortality, as no woman would ever be strong enough to kill him.

Emboldened by the boon, he amassed a formidable army of the mightiest *Asuras* in the world and commanded them to attack the earth and heaven. Indra and the *devas* fought hard to retain their heaven but *Mahisha's* hordes were too powerful for them. Since *Mahisha* could not be slain by the *devas*, he couldn't be defeated in any duel and he overpowered all of them easily. He banished them from heaven and established his authority over all three spheres.

He tormented the worshippers of the *devas* on earth as he believed that the gods drew strength from their offerings and prayers. He mercilessly ordered the slaying of all *rishis* who worshipped any deity but him. He believed himself to be the Supreme Lord of the Universe and paid obeisance to none. His atrocities were unbearable to his victims who cried out in anguish to the *devas*.

The *devas*, themselves his victims, had no option but to turn to the Creator who had bestowed such strength on *Mahishaasura*. Lord Brahma, however, was helpless as he could not go against his own boon and therefore asked them to go to *Vaikuntha*, the abode of Lord Vishnu. He too accompanied them. In *Vaikuntha*, the group of deities poured out their woes to the Supreme One.

Lord Vishnu was lost in thought. He knew that there was no woman in the three worlds capable of overpowering *Mahisha*. Thus, they went to *Kailasa*, the mountain home of Lord Shiva and His consort Parvati to seek their counsel. When all the gods assembled and recounted their tale of suffering at the hands of *Mahisha* and described their helplessness, Lord Shiva was furious. He seethed in anger and from his being, there emanated a radiance.

Soon, the fury of Lord Vishnu, Lord Brahma and all the other gods too, manifested in the form of radiance. Rays of light from their beings converged on the earth in the hermitage of the sage

Kaatyan. From the convergence of the light that emanated from all gods, arose Durga. She was a manifestation of the *Shakti* of all the celestial beings, a manifestation of the Supreme Power, of Energy. She was the governing force of all the universe, in the form of an eight-armed woman of great beauty and she was mounted on a lion.

The gods descended to the hermitage of *Kaatyayan* and they paid obeisance to Her. They sang her praises and each gave her a symbol of their might. Thus, Lord Vishnu gave her the *Sudarshana Chakra*, Lord Shiva gave the *Trishula*, his trident spear, Lord Brahma gave the *Kamandala* that held the water of Ganga, Indra gave her his *Vajra*, the thunderbolt and the other gods too gave her their weapons.

They named her *Kaatyaayani*, the daughter of *Kaatyayan*. Armed with their weapons and heady with their songs of her praise, Durga let out a laugh. Immediately, her lion let out an earth-shattering roar. Wasting no time, she rode out to meet her destined foe.

Reaching *Mahisha's* capital, she again let out a laugh. The ground shook beneath her and *Mahisha*, on his throne, was rattled. Durga proclaimed in his city that she wanted to challenge him to a fight. *Mahisha* was greatly amused. He was smitten by her immense beauty but was enraged by her desire to want to fight him.

Did she, a mere woman, stand any chance against him, the Supreme Lord of the universe? He thought of her as an brazen fool and decided to teach her a lesson. He sent out his troops to humour her. He ordered them to subdue her and bring her to him. His hordes rode out to meet her in combat but she decimated them in no time. She laughed as she killed each one of them. When *Mahisha* learned of their defeat, he became furious and ordered his most powerful soldiers to go and capture her. However, Durga welcomed all of them with death. She created replicas of herself and her army soon killed all of *Mahisha's* soldiers.

Then *Mahishasura* decided that it was time that he crushed her himself. He donned his armour and armed himself as he rode out to face his adversary. His mind was so full of rage that not once did he pause to consider if Durga could be the woman to bring about his downfall. When at last he saw her, she was alone. All the other

Durgas had withdrawn into Her, having decimated *Mahishaasura's* army. Seeing him approach, Durga laughed insultingly. She was intoxicated by her victories in the battle. She disregarded *Mahishaasura's* snorts and roars of fury that would have struck terror in the hearts of others. Her lion, equally intoxicated, roared at *Mahisha* mockingly.

She announced to him, "Wicked *Mahisha*! Vile *Mahisha*! *Mahishaasura*, the tormentor of all the worlds! In your great ignorance, you asked the Creator to grant you death only at the hands of a woman, a being you had utter disregard for. You never thought a woman could ever overpower you and having received the boon, you believed yourself virtually immortal. Behold me now, evil *Asura*! I am Durga, the manifestation of *Shakti*. I have come to slay you and rid the universe of your malice." Her words only infuriated *Mahisha* more. Blinded by rage, he took the form of a massive buffalo, stomped menacingly and then rushed to tackle her lion. The lion deftly dodged him and Durga slashed out at him with her sword.

However, *Mahisha* transformed himself into an elephant using his powers of sorcery and charged at Durga, whipping her with his mighty trunk. Durga grabbed him by one of his tusks and dashed him to the ground. He changed form yet again and became a lion as fierce as Durga's. The two lions pounced on each other, their paws slashing each others' faces. Durga's lion overpowered *Mahisha* but he escaped and took on the form of a buffalo once more. This time, Durga tamed the raging buffalo with a noose and then beheaded the beast. From its torso, *Mahisha* began to emerge in human form but Durga's lion, sturdy as the Himalaya mountains, pounced on him and pinned him to the ground as Durga raised her trident and pierced the chest of the evil *Mahishaasura*, slaying him.

Then she rode back to the heavens, her lion roaring fiercely and the reinstated *devas* all sang hymns in her praise. They named her as *Mashishaasura-Mardhini*. She who slew *Mahishaasura*.

Durga Puja - the ceremonial worship of the mother goddess, is one of the most important festivals of India. Apart from being a religious festival, it is also an occasion for reunion and rejuvenation, and a celebration of traditional culture and customs. While the rituals entail ten days of fast, feast and worship, the last four days - *Saptami*, *Ashtami*, *Navami* and *Dashami* - are celebrated with much gaiety and grandeur in India and abroad, especially in Bengal, where the ten-armed goddess riding the lion is worshipped with great passion and devotion.

Durga Puja is celebrated every year in the Hindu month of *Ashwin* (September-October) and commemorates Prince Rama's invocation of the goddess before going to war with the demon king *Ravana*. Thus goes the story of Lord Rama, who first worshipped the '*Mahishasura Mardini*' or the slayer of the buffalo-demon, by offering 108 blue lotuses and lighting 108 lamps, at this time of the year.

Guru Nanak

Jai Ram, Guru Nanak's brother-in-law was serving as the *dewan* (steward) to the governor, Nawab Daulat Khan Lodhi of Sultanpur. It is said that both Jai Ram and Rai Bular opined that Guru Nanak was a saint ill-treated by his father and thus Jai Ram promised to find a job for him in Sultanpur.

Guru Nanak's sister, Bebi Nanaki, was deeply devoted to her younger brother. On their annual visit to Talwandi, when she noticed her father's impatience at her brother's indifference towards worldly activities, she decided to take him to Sultanpur. Her father consented, hoping that he would choose a good profession.

Jai Ram got the Guru the post of a store-keeper at the Nawab's state granary, where the grain was collected as a part of land revenue, and later sold. The Guru carried out the duties of the store-keeper very efficiently. The minstrel Mardana, subsequently joined the Guru and other friends too followed. Guru Nanak introduced them to the Governor, who provided them suitable jobs in his administration.

Every night there was Shabad-Kirtan (singing of the divine). One day he was weighing provisions and was counting each weighing as 'One, two, three... ten, eleven, twelve, thirteen'. When he reached the number thirteen (13)- *'Tera'* (in Punjabi language Tera means number 13, and Tera also means 'yours', that is 'I am Yours, O Lord'), he slipped into a meditative state.

Guru Nanak went on weighing by saying, "Tera, tera, tera..." Customers were pleased to receive extra provisions and did not know how to carry so many goods. They could not understand the bounties of the Lord.

Ultimately the message reached Nawab Daulat Khan when a charge was levied against the Guru that he was recklessly giving away the grain. The Nawab ordered an inquiry which was conducted meticulously. The Guru's detractors were surprised when the stores were found to be in order. In fact, the accounts showed surplus grain stocks in favour of Guru Nanak.

When there is deep devotion and alertness, what opens in you is 'tera', meaning 'I am yours, Oh, God'.

You should be open to the miracles of life.

A Sufi Thought

A group of frogs were moving in the woods. Of these, two fell into a deep pit. The other frogs gathered around the pit. When they saw how deep the pit was, they told the unfortunate frogs that they would never be able to get out. The two frogs ignored their comments and tried to jump up out of the pit.

The other frogs kept telling them to stop and that they were as good as dead. Finally, one of the frogs paid heed to what the other frogs were saying and simply gave up. He fell and died.

The other frog continued to jump as hard as he could. Once again, the crowd of frogs yelled at him to stop the pain and suffering and just die. He jumped even harder and finally made it out. When he got out, the other frogs asked him, "Why did you continue jumping? Didn't you hear us?"

The frog informed them that he was deaf. He'd thought they were encouraging him to try and jump out, all that while.

This story has the following lessons:-

There's a power of life and death in the tongue. An encouraging word to someone who is down can lift her up and help her sail through the day.

A destructive word to someone who is down might be what it takes to kill her. Be careful as to what you say. Infuse life in those who cross your path.

The power of words... it's sometimes hard to understand that an encouraging word can go such a long way. Anyone can speak words that tend to rob others of the spirit to prevail in difficult times.

Special is the individual who takes the time to encourage another.

Syat Vaada of Jainism

Syat Vaada is one of the beautiful tenets of Jainism. To the true practitioner of this tenet, its beauty is revealed as 'inner freedom'.

Syat Vaada teaches you that everything is relative, nothing is absolute. For example, if you tell a Syat Vaada practitioner that some person is stupid, he will tell you that the stupidity is relative and not absolute. One who understands the theory of relativity will not be a victim of absolutism.

Whenever you form an opinion of another and consider that as absolute, then you stop seeing that other person as a flowing being. No one is static, everyone is a flowing being. Considering any individual in the absolute sense destroys the basic quality of an individual as a flowing being. The quality of your life depends on the quality of your relationships. Keeping the perception of your relationships relative, is what keeps it open. Openness ventilates life.

Quite often, you are a prisoner of your own knowledge. When you say, 'as far as I know' you do not consider your knowledge to be absolute. Simultaneously, you do not erase whatever you know and remain open to other variables. In the process, you set yourself and others free, by not labelling others. If you label others, you see them only as labels, not as persons. This is an ignorant way of living.

Jainism teaches to live a life based on this principle and be wise. A wise person spreads happiness all around while an unwise one distributes unhappiness!

Syat Vaada, when applied creatively in life, can mean something like this –

Eg. If you term someone as stupid, it only means:-

◆ As far as I know, that person is stupid;

◆ Upto a point, that person is stupid; or

◆ To me, that person is stupid.

This does not authorise you to address anyone in absolute term, but only in relative terms.

Another important aspect of Jainism is non-violence. The practice of non-violence in the truest terms means not hurting anyone or anything intentionally either by thought or action. This is a very important dimension in one's growth in spirituality.

A Powerful Zoroastrian Thought

There are many lores as to how the Zoroastrians who are also known as Parsis, were allowed to settle in India.

When they landed at Sanjan, on the shores of what is now the modern day Gujarat, somewhere between the 8th and 10th Century CE, their priestly leaders were brought before the local ruler, Jadi or Jadhav Rana, who presented them a vessel "brimful" of milk to signify that the surrounding lands could not possibly accommodate any more people.

The Parsi head priest responded by adding sugar to the milk to symbolise how the immigrants would blend with the local community. They assured that they would mingle with the locals, like sugar dissolves in the milk, sweetening the society but not unsettling it.

Jadi responded to their symbolic gesture and granted the immigrants land and permission to practice their religion, unhindered, if they would lay down their arms, adopt local dress, respect local customs, conduct weddings and other ceremonies only at night, and learn the local language, Gujarati.

True to their promise, Parsis, as a community, have made the country proud in all walks of life.

Jesus and the Mustard Seeds

Jesus told the crowd another story. He said, "The kingdom of heaven is like a mustard seed. Someone took the seed and planted it in a field. It is the smallest of all your seeds. But when it grows, it is the largest of all garden plants. It becomes a tree. Birds come and rest in its branches."

When you hear the word mustard, you probably think of the spicy yellow stuff you put on a hot dog. That is the same kind of mustard. People use mustard as a spice, and when they grind up mustard seed and mix it with water or vinegar, we get ketchup's best friend. (We believe the Romans were the first people to make prepared mustard, so it is possible that Jesus ate mustard similar to ours!)

The mustard seed is one of the smallest seeds. But when it is planted in the ground, it grows up to be one of the largest plants. It can grow up to 12 feet tall. That's twice as tall as a grown man! It can look more like a tree than a plant. As Jesus said, even birds come and rest in its branches.

The seed starts out very small, but it is very powerful. Within the seed is the ability to grow an enormous plant. The growth is slow and steady. If you looked at it every day, you might not see much change. But if you planted the seed, walked away, and then came back in one year, you would see a huge change! The seed would become an enormous plant, bearing fruit and providing a place of rest for the birds. Just try to imagine a plant, 12 feet tall and 6 feet wide, all packed into this tiny seed! Now that is one powerful seed.

How is this like the kingdom of God? Well, we can look at this parable in two ways. In the big picture, this parable explains the kingdom of God worldwide. And at a more personal level, this story brings out that the kingdom of God is within each believer.

The people that Jesus was speaking to were Jewish. Remember, the Jews were God's chosen people. Through the years, God promised that He was going to send a man to save them. The people misunderstood what this meant. They thought God would send a king to rescue them from the Roman rule. They expected the Saviour to set them free with military force. But that was not at all what God had planned. God sent the Saviour to save them from their own sin.

With this parable, Jesus was telling His listeners that their way was not God's way at all. God's way was meek. The Saviour, Jesus, came as a newborn baby. He grew up as a carpenter's son. He quietly stepped onto the scene. He spoke out to small groups of people, and then more and more people came to listen. He had a small group of followers at first. Without much warning, the kingdom began to grow as people put their trust in Jesus.

After Jesus' death and resurrection, a handful of disciples were left to spread the truth of God's kingdom. They were like that tiny seed. In the huge population of the entire world, they were a little speck. But just like that mustard seed, they were full of hidden power. They had God's Holy Spirit in them. As the disciples travelled and taught, the number of people who believed grew. Worldwide, the kingdom continued to grow. Just like the mustard plant produces more seeds for planting, the disciples made more disciples. The disciples' disciples made disciples. Just like the mustard plant grows tall and wide, the kingdom of God spread in every direction. God's kingdom continues to grow even today.

When Jesus taught this parable, God's kingdom on earth consisted of only a few ragged fishermen. But in time, the kingdom has grown to reach nearly every single nation. It has grown just as Jesus said it would!

The Kingdom of Heaven is within you! Discover it.

Buddha and the Mustard Seeds

During Buddha's time, there lived a woman named Kisa Gotami. She married young and gave birth to a son. One day, the baby fell sick and died soon after. Kisa Gotami loved her son greatly and refused to believe that her son was dead. She carried the body of her son around her village, asking if there was anyone who could bring her son back to life.

The villagers all saw that the son was already dead and there was nothing that could be done. They advised her to accept his death and make arrangements for the funeral.

In great grief, she fell upon her knees and clutched her son's body close to her. She kept pleading her son to wake up.

A village elder took pity on her and suggested that she consult the Buddha.

"Kisa Gotami. We cannot help you. But you should go to the Buddha. Maybe he can bring your son back to life!"

Kisa Gotami was extremely excited on hearing the elder's words. She immediately went to the Buddha's residence and pleaded him to bring her son back to life.

"Kisa Gotami, I might be able to bring your son back to life, provided you do as I say."

"My Lord, I'm willing to do anything to bring my son back."

"If so, I would like you to fetch me something. Get me a mustard seed. Remember, however, that the seed is brought from a house, where none residing there has ever lost a family member. Go fetch this seed and your son shall rise to life."

Having great faith in the Buddha's promise, Kisa Gotami went from house to house, looking for the mustard seed.

At the first house, a young woman offered to give her some mustard seeds. But when Kisa Gotami asked if she had ever lost a family member to death, the young women said her grandmother died a few months ago.

Kisa Gotami thanked the young woman and explained why the mustard seeds did not meet the Buddha's requirements.

She moved on to the 2nd house. A husband died a few years back. The 3rd house lost an uncle and the 4th house lost an aunt. She kept moving from house to house but the answer was all the same – every house had lost some family member to death.

Kisa Gotami finally realised that there was none in this world who had never lost some family member to death. She understood that death is an inevitable and natural part of life.

Putting aside her grief, she buried her son in the forest. She then returned to the Buddha and became his follower.

Significance of Mantras

Life consists of both, organised as well as disorganised aspects. Mantras help us, in mystical ways, to transform the disorganised to organised aspects, guiding us out of unhealthy stress to healthy stress.

Mantras are the verbal stimulation of the soul through sound energy. It is said that nothing impacts the mind as much as sound does. We experience sound in various forms. At one end there is jarring noise, at the other, is the harmony of music. Sound is also the perception of silence – the interlude between one node of sound and another. To a mind in distress, nothing is more musical than silence. There is music in silence and it requires a trained or disciplined mind to perceive it.

'Heard melodies are sweet, but those unheard are sweeter.' (John Keats, Ode on a Grecian Urn)

Experience, especially divine, cannot be captured through sensory perceptions. Mantras help us in this aspect. Reciting or chanting Mantras, meaningfully and with devotion, can lead one to a new world of experience; a world, that surpasses what is perceived through the best of logic or intellectual effort.

Mantras are insightful inputs that *rishis* (great seers) have handed down to us. Conditioning themselves through penance, shedding all their material linkages with living, they handed down their experience to mankind at large, in the form of Mantras. It is said that the best way to learn Mantras, is through a Guru. *Paramatma* – the God touches our soul, through a Guru, by way of a Mantra.

Om

Every vibration has a related sound. Everything in the universe has vibration and thus, has sound as an intrinsic attribute. Each atom, molecule, cell, object, a group of objects, the entire universe too, has a vibrational link and thereby, a unique sound.

When you chant a mantra, you merge with the sound vibration and resonate with the energy wavelength of the object of your mantra. Mantra chanting unifies you with each of those, elsewhere, who is chanting that mantra and also with everyone who has chanted the mantra at any time. All saints who have ever reached enlightenment through the technique of chanting that mantra connect with you as you connect with the vibration of the mantra. You merge with their purified and holy quintessence and you become pure and holy because that divine level of existence vibrates only with holiness, peace, and bliss.

By chanting a mantra, your cells, molecules, atoms, and sub-atomic particles all vibrate at the same wavelength as that of the mantra. Once attuned to this vibration you connect with everything resonating on that plane of existence. It's like tuning a radio. At first, you may get static, but once you are in the right frequency your reception is perfect. Om is the universal sound. It is within every word and within everything. As such, when you chant Om, you merge with all energy and all forms, from the sub-atomic to the universal, from the grossest to the most divine. And when you are tuned in perfectly, you will receive holy frequencies clearly and merge and emerge as one with the source of all, to live happily.

Many meditation teachers suggest that it is necessary to understand every intellectual aspect of the meaning of the mantra that is being practised, but just as many others feel that the intellect may tend to confuse and hold back spiritual progress. What both types of teachers agree upon, is that mantras have the potential to take its practitioners to the level of consciousness that transcend the limitations of the mind by a billion-fold. There is an ancient tale that very well shows that true devotion and complete absorption is the key.

Once upon a time in a land far away lived a poor uneducated, mentally challenged man who tended a herd of cows for his master. He happened to meet a meditation teacher and was amazed at his calm, loving, gentle and happy nature. He longed to know that experience which made the teacher who he was, first-hand. Thereby, he went to the teacher and begged him to teach him a way to achieve the inner peace that radiated from the teacher. The teacher accepted him as his disciple but soon found out that the man couldn't understand any of the philosophical points that he was making. In fact, the disciple couldn't even remember the mantra 'Om' when it was taught to him.

The teacher lovingly said, "My son, you don't seem to know anything at all; you can't be taught, and can't remember anything. You are devoted and sincere in your desire to gain happiness though, so I will try to help you. My son, what do you know?"

The man said, "Oh! great teacher, the only thing I know is cows. All my life I've spent caring for cows, making sure they graze, are milked, and are kept clean. Yes, for me, cows are everything." "Well, that's alright," said the teacher, "then you know what sound the cows make." "Oh yes," said the man, "they say moo." "Very well then," said the teacher, "for you, moo will be your mantra. All you have to do is say moo continually and you will reach freedom from suffering and experience true bliss." So, the man chanted moo, moo, moo when he took the cows out to graze and he chanted moo, moo, moo when he milked them, and he chanted moo, moo, moo when he cleaned them. He chanted moo all the time and very soon merged with that vibration, which is Om backwards, reached the highest peak of joyous understanding and lived happily thereafter.

From this story, we learn that it is virtually impossible to chant Om "wrong". It is, after all, an insentient sound. But the giver of this sound to the universe knows the intention and devotion of the practitioner and that is by what we are rewarded. It is said that a minute of sincere chanting is superior to a thousand hours of the mere reciting of the words. A parrot can be taught to recite a mantra, but this will just be vibrations in the air. It is the love and worship behind the sound that counts.

Technically though, there is a "correct" way to chant 'Om'. It is made up of three letters: A, U, M. These contain all the sounds there are. The A is guttural and comes from the throat. It is pronounced without any part of the tongue or palate in contact. The U sound comes from the middle of the sounding board, the palate. In Sanskrit, the A and U combine to become O. The O sound is vibrated from the navel / solar plexus area and sent up the sternum to the voice region, the lips, where the M sound is prolonged and vibrated into the crown of the head. This vibrating M is felt in every cell of the body and is beamed out lovingly, soothingly, powerfully, to everything, everyone, everywhere. Intellectually and metaphysically, A stands for the physical world perceptible to the senses, the material world. U represents the astral and dream planes, heaven and hell. M is the unknown, deep sleep, and that which is unfathomable to the intellect. Thus 'Om' contains the entire spectrum of sound, words, worlds, and concepts. 'Om' is the source of all light, love, and wisdom.

There are three ways to chant the mantra - loud, soft i.e., with gentle lip movements or by humming the mantra, and completely silent i.e., within oneself. When done aloud and particularly when done with others, the sound of 'Om' is energising, calming, and healing. Although it is often encouraged to chant the mantra at all times, it would certainly be questionable to consider chanting 'Om' aloud in the middle of a board meeting. Similarly, it may be preferable to chant 'Om' silently just by moving your lips if you are in a movie theatre. Chanting 'Om' completely silently is considered the most potent method because it is not dependent on having a human voice box, or lips, or facial muscles, all of which are temporary manifestations compared to the billions of years that you will be fully at one with Om.

It is advantageous in spiritual development when you consider the theological, philosophical and mystical aspects of 'Om' that accrue when chanting with your physical eyes closed, looking through the third eye, and focussing on your breath. This may seem complex and complicated, but once in sync, it comes naturally, as 'Om' reveals your 'True Self', to you.

Practice

Sit in a comfortable position keeping the back erect. Take a deep breath and chant 'Om' (Om is a composite of A, U and M).

While chanting, focus on the sound 'U' in 'Om'.

By doing so, the mind is focused and stilled.

While exhaling, 'Om' should be chanted. Observe navel centre being pulled in while chanting 'Om'. This is a mystic centre. The navel centre is a source of connection with one's mother, hence it is known as a mystic centre.

So, inhale and exhale chanting 'Om'. Feel the vibration of 'U' while chanting. Feel the navel is pulled in while chanting. This has to be done minimum ten times in a single sitting.

In the process, discover a mysterious spiritual centre.

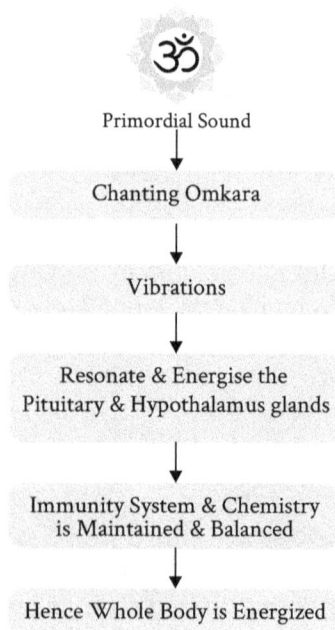

ॐ

Primordial Sound

↓

Chanting Omkara

↓

Vibrations

↓

Resonate & Energise the
Pituitary & Hypothalamus glands

↓

Immunity System & Chemistry
is Maintained & Balanced

↓

Hence Whole Body is Energized

Uncovering Your True Self

What is the nature of this elusive 'self' that you wish to understand? Have you ever asked yourself as to what you are really made of?

According to our ancient scriptures, we are a combination of three things: the gross body, the subtle body and the causal body. Each body is covered by sheaths (*koshas*). These are — *annamaya, pranamaya, manonmaya, vignanamaya and Anandamaya*. As we embark on the journey within, we would uncover these layers.

Annamaya (the Physical Body)

This is the physical body that you can touch, feel and see. It is the layer of skin, muscle tissue and bones. It harmonises your first *kosha*. Through the practice of yoga, you first explore this layer and understand it well. The right eating for the right body energy is very important. Good exercise for one hour a day is necessary. One's being healthy, is equally important too.

Pranamaya (the Breath or Life Force)

Prana is the energy for all kinds of motion. It exists and pervades throughout the universe and in all things. Where there is no *prana*, no activity takes place. It is a field, a subtle and measurable form of energy. You should spend at least half an hour a day on *pranayama*. As a breathing exercise, *pranayama* makes *pranic* energy permeate each and every cell in the body.

Manomaya (the Mental Sheath)

The mind, as consciousness, is a field of energy by itself. Whenever possible, keep your mind free of thoughts. For example, you may be driving a car, but your mind would be engaged in analysing the reasons for your boss's unusual outburst that morning. If there were to be an gadget to record all that we said and thought, we would be convinced of our own madness! There is no coherence in our words and our thoughts jump endlessly from one topic to another. It is as if we were set to prove the essential correctness of the psychologist's observation: there are only two kinds of people, the insane and the more insane.

You overcome this tendency by practising *manonmaya* – mental serenity. When you are driving a car, keep your mind calm and collected. When you want to talk, you use your thought.

Vijnanamaya (the Intellectual Aura)
The ability to use thought in a proactive and exploring mode is the concentration of a creative energy.

Your thinking can be empty, argumentative or justifying or breakthrough in character. If one can initiate one's thinking to the breakthrough mode, it unlocks the intellectual body.

Anandamaya (the Blissful State)
Bliss, i.e. *Ananda* is a unique word in Sanskrit. *Ananda* has no opposites in Sanskrit. Like has its opposite in dislike, pleasure is the opposite of pain, the day has night but *Ananda* has no such opposite. Hence *Ananda* is cause-less. If one is causelessly blissful there is an experience of fullness. That fullness, is the moment of *Ananda*.

Body Energy

Food Energy

Thought Energy

Emotional Energy

Silence Energy

Who in your organisation can see the echo principle...like Ambarisha whose narration is given below? Can you also see how Lord Vishnu conserved his energy by not getting hurt?

Conserve your energy by not wasting through getting hurt, upset or ego.

Reflect on this story from Indian mythology.

There lived a king named Ambarisha. He always meditated and prayed to Lord Vishnu. On one occasion, he continued his prayer for three days and for those three days, he fasted, neither eating a grain of food nor drinking a drop of water. After three days, he invited all the priests. Soon all of them had gathered and King Ambarisha was busy serving food, gifts and alms.

But, all of a sudden, Rishi Durvasa came to the spot. He was a very learned but very short tempered rishi. King Ambarisha welcomed the great ascetic.

"I am indeed blessed by your presence," King Ambarisha said. "Please partake of the lunch to be served and give your blessings to me."

Rishi Durvasa said, "First I must go and have a bath in the river nearby before I take any food." Rishi Durvasa, left for the river to have a dip. Everyone waited for his return. Hours went by and time was passing by.

One of the old priests said, "Oh! king, you must break your fast before noon."

"Respected priest how can I do so?" King Ambarisha asked. "Rishi Durvasa is my guest and everyone knows of his foul temper. If I don't wait till his return and eat before that, he will surely be very annoyed."

One of the priests suggested, "You can drink water to break the fast before noon and you can eat something on Rishi Durvasa return. This way you won't sin and you won't insult the Rishi either."

King Ambarisha agreed and took a glass of water and was about to drink it when Rishi Durvasa came back. He turned red in his face with anger. "Ambarisha, how dare you drink before serving me?" He exclaimed in anger. "Respected Rishi, I have not broken the fast. We may begin our lunch together," King Ambarisha explained.

"You'll be punished for your doing. You don't even know how to treat a guest," saying so, Rishi Durvasa plucked some hair from his beard and made a chakra from it.

The chakra raced towards king Ambarisha to cut off his neck. King Ambarisha prayed to Lord Vishnu for help. Lord Vishnu heard his devotee's cry for help and sent his own chakra in defence. Rishi

Durvasa's chakra got destroyed and the Lord Vishnu's chakra started chasing Rishi Durvasa. He started running to save himself. He crossed river and hills and ran through caves but the chakra kept following him.

Rishi Durvasa ran to Lord Shiva and said, "Lord Shiva, please save my life from the Vishnu chakra."

"Go away from here. You have insulted Lord Vishnu's devotee, so the Lord is angry. I cannot help you at all," Lord Shiva replied.

Helpless Rishi Durvasa went to Lord Brahma for help. Lord Brahma said, "It's Lord Vishnu's chakra. Go to him for help. I have nothing to do with all this."

So Durvasa went to Lord Vishnu and bowed before him saying, "O Lord, please save me from your chakra."

Lord Vishnu said, "You have been rude to my devotee. You have no control over your anger. Don't come to me with apologies. You have been rude to Ambarisha, go to him. You have insulted him and only his forgiveness will save you from my chakra."

At last Rishi, Durvasa ran to King Ambarisha. Reaching King Ambarisha, he said. "Ambarisha, I am sorry for my rude behaviour. Please save my life, it is in your hands. Please forgive me and stop the Vishnu chakra."

King Ambarisha prayed to Lord Vishnu to take back his chakra. Instantly, the Vishnu chakra vanished.

Rishi Durvasa heaved a sigh of relief. Then he asked King Ambarisha, "I went to Lord Shiva, Lord Brahma and Lord Vishnu but no one could stop the Vishnu chakra from chasing me. What power did you have to stop it?"

I have the power of Lord Vishnu's love for me. That's what helped me to rid you of the chasing Vishnu chakra."

It is seen from above, Lord Brahma, Lord Shiva and Lord Vishnu – all with strong energy pockets could not undo the wrong. Ultimately Lord Vishnu advised Rishi Durvasa that Ambarisha's forgiveness was only the solution.

This is a case where all the five *koshas* in a person are open, as an organised body.

So, there is a need for organised self, hence start with the purification of five *Koshas.*

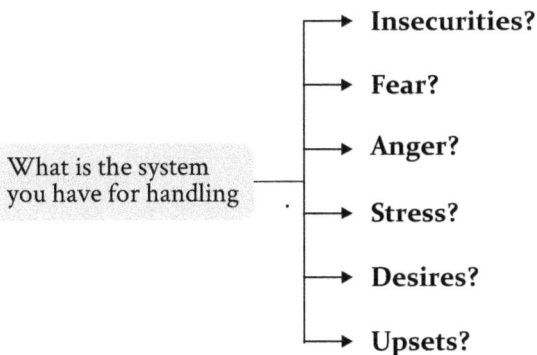

What is the system you have for handling

- → **Insecurities?**
- → **Fear?**
- → **Anger?**
- → **Stress?**
- → **Desires?**
- → **Upsets?**

There is also a case where all five *koshas* were not open as in the case of Vishwamithra mentioned in the earlier chapter, thus as an unorganised body.

Reflection Point

Will you operate your spiritual key in a situation like this?

The Freedom Within
– a Different Kind of Independence

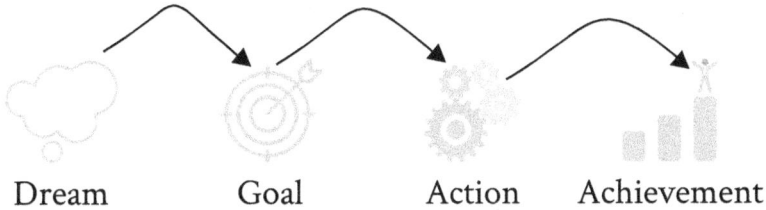

Dream   Goal   Action   Achievement

The year 1765 marked the start of India's territorial dominion under the British Empire. On August 15, 1947, nearly 200 years later, India gained independence from that rule. What is remarkable about our struggle for freedom is that we fought not with weapons, but through non-violent resistance. It was an unprecedented occurrence in human history that such resistance could free us from one of the most powerful empires of the world. Where weapons failed, non-violence succeeded.

Instrumental to its success was Mahatma Gandhi, the protagonist of Indian Independence Movement. What motivated Mahatma Gandhi in the seemingly impossible quest for freedom? He based many of his own personal principles and philosophies on the teachings of the Bhagavad Gita. 'The Bhagavad Gita is not only my Bible and my Koran, it is more than that, it is my mother.' Mahatma Gandhi turned to it in his most trying moments.

While the Father of the Nation played such a large role in its gaining freedom, he also firmly believed in the importance of inner freedom. 'As human beings, our greatness lies not so much in being able to remake the world – that is the myth of the atomic age – as in being able to remake ourselves'.

The words of the Bhagavad Gita speak as to how to 'remake ourselves'. They speak of a different form of freedom. A freedom from suffering and illusion. As I repeatedly say:

"You are suffering not because of difficulties. You are suffering because of your internal hurts. On the battlefield in the Mahabharata, Lord Krishna heals Arjuna's wounds and when the wound is healed, Arjuna's action is very different.

That's the context of the Bhagavad Gita. The Bhagavad Gita also says, very clearly, to Arjuna, 'Be careful what your beliefs are.' Your beliefs are going to change the quality of your life. If you believe that God 'will help me at the right time', at his biding, then nothing will shake you."

The mind can make a heaven and a hell of our lives. "The Bhagavad Gita tells us, the Upanishads tell us that there is sufficiency in the world, but the trouble is one feels deficient inside. Since there is a deficiency in us, even when we look at sufficiency, we see only deficiency."

If we keep our minds rooted in positivity and learn to look at difficulties as challenges, not as problems, we will find our own freedom from suffering.

Mahatma Gandhi gives one more suggestion to finding ourselves and our inner freedom: 'The best way to find yourself, is to lose yourself in the service of others'. As India begins yet another year of independence, it may be wise to heed the words of the man who fought so dearly for it. Let us all work to serve our country and pursue our own inner freedom by being open and learning constantly.

Here is an interesting message that I recently received. I feel it is very appropriate to imbibe in each one of our lives.

The prayer that God answered for you is the same prayer others have been praying but without success.

Be grateful.

The road you use safely on a daily basis is the same road where many others have lost their precious lives.

Be grateful.

The temple in which God blessed you is the same temple that other people too worship in, but their lives are yet in disarray.

Be grateful.

The qualification that gave you a job is the same qualification that someone else too has, but that someone still does not have a job.

Be grateful.

That hospital bed on which you were healed and discharged, is the same bed where many others breathed their last.

Be grateful.

The rain that made your field produce good crops is the same rain that devastated someone else's field.

Be grateful.

Be grateful because whatever you have is not by your power, your might, your talent or your qualifications, but it's just the "Grace of God."

He is the giver of everything you have.

For everything you have, be grateful.

With Love and Blessings
Poojya Sukhabodhananda

We are grateful for the loving support of

Late Shri. Chempi Venkatesh Bhat
and Late Smt. Padmavathi Bhat,

in bringing out this book.

Icon Glossary

A catalogue of 'Icons' used in this book. The icons make it easy to flag key concepts in the book.

Icons with Label	A Brief Description
Success Mantra	The key idea for success in a para or chapter – a ready reference and motivational tool.
Light Unto Oneself *(To know more, rea• the story at the en• of this section)*	Aimed towards helping you work out a personal framework, to iron out the errors in your personality or living. Understand and correct the concept logically as an intellectual framework. Internally feel the concept rightly and correct as an emotional framework.
Outside In the intellectual framework **Inside Out** the emotional framework	The wise harmony of *Outsi•e In,* that is *the intellectual framework* and *Insi•e Out,* that is *the emotional framework* and balancing these two will lead you to discover an effective source of vibrant energies.
Reflection Point	An uplifting idea — ponder for deeper assimilation.
Spiritual Key *(To know more, rea• the story at the en• of this section)*	A key idea in a chapter, constructed from philosophy.

Icons with Label	A Brief Description
Mythology	Relevant, time-tested stories to lead you to a key idea.
Case Study	Drawing from modern management methodologies, illustrations from current life-space.
Story	A popular mode to breakdown complex concepts and draw the essence.
Nyaya *(To know more, rea* the story at the en* of this section)*	Maxims from ancient Sanskrit literature which give a balanced approach to Life.

Leadership qualities coupled with key characteristics or values to take you to profitable growth. A spiritual formula transforming frustration to fascination, that can be used to solve your problem. *(To know more, rea* the lea*ership tips at the en* of this section)*

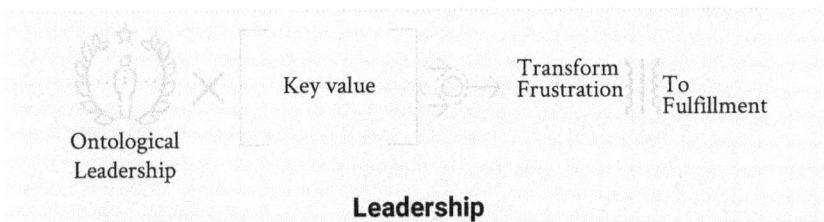

Ontological Leadership $\times$ Key value $\rightarrow$ Transform Frustration → To Fulfillment

Leadership

Light Unto Oneself

Raghav lost his eyesight in a freak accident. The loss of sight, however, was no setback for him. His environment was supportive, and he was financially well-off. His wife and four children made life comfortable for him.

He was a miser though. Never splurged and looked closely at utility whenever he had to spend.

His childhood friend, Shivpal, an NRI, called on him for a courtesy visit. He was a well-known eye surgeon, in the US and, having heard of Raghav's mishap, Shivpal wanted to examine him to see if there was a way out.

And, there was! Shivpal advised that a simple transplant surgery, costing some Rs. 5 lakhs, could restore his sight. Shivpal also offered to talk to good surgeons in town, to have the operation done locally. Raghav said he'd need a couple of days to decide.

Rs. 5 lakhs and the sight would return, is this worth it? "Why waste money when I have a family of many members with so many eyes," was his logic.

He had always taken pride that his wife's eyes were his window to light. Then, there were his four, loving children. So five pairs of eyes out of six, in his family, functioned – was the sixth required? He called Shivpal, thanked him and said no.

Everything went well for a while. One day, when Raghav was resting, a fire broke out. In the panic, everyone but Raghav ran out of the house. None realised - Raghav was sleeping inside and his cries for help proved to be of no avail.

The family lamented - if only Raghav had heeded to his friend's advice, he would have survived that fire. His eyes would have given him light, in that needful hour. Darkness always surrounded him as he banked on others' help. Without own visual support, he struggled in the end.

Look at the foolish logic that made him dependent and crippled.

Similarly, are you a victim of your foolish logic?

Why don't we practice the essence learnt from talks, books, stories and real-life instances? A pupil once told his Master, "Reading certain books motivates me. But, with the passage of time, the motivation wanes. What should I do?"

"Be a lantern. Be a light unto yourself. Awaken the inner eyes to serve as your light."

Spiritual Key

Mary and Paul, a lovely couple, were seen as icons of marital harmony in the neighbourhood. They loved and trusted each other, immensely. They were married to each other for more than a decade, with no offspring.

They were happy until Mary landed in jail. Sadly, for a crime that she hadn't committed.

Paul tried to help out. He hired a good advocate. The evidence, however, was loaded against Mary and she had to face jail. Paul refused to give up though. He knew that Mary was not a criminal. He visited her daily at the prison and asked her not to lose hope. He was sure that they could appeal to the higher court and she'd be out of jail soon.

Mary could see that Paul was stressed. He was trying to help out as he trusted her but in the bargain, was running himself down. His health was at stake. Yes, she hadn't committed a crime. But, unable to bear the thought of Paul fighting a losing battle, she lied to Paul that she'd committed the crime. She wanted her husband to be free from any tension. Paul, however, was unconvinced. He assured Mary that he'd get her out at any cost. Deep within in his heart, he was sure that Mary had not committed the crime.

He did something interesting. He looked for an expert on jail escape plans. The expert told Paul that all the prisons however secure would always have some weak point. That would be the key to escape from jail. The expert added, 'Be alert at all times. Look for an opening. You'll soon find one key to escape.'

Paul pondered over the expert's advice. Soon, he found a good idea, a way for Mary to escape from the jail.

In life too, one is trapped in a psychological prison, making it appear like it's impossible to come out of it. Like Mary and Paul, using your 100 inner eyes, you will see a path to walk out of the inner prison. You will discover the key to inner freedom.

You'll see a way out if you look carefully.

Arjuna faced a mighty army consisting of his great-grandfather and guru, opposing him in the Mahabharata war. He was in a psychological prison of his own thoughts. He further sugarcoated his despair as *vairagya* or delusion.

Lord Krishna helped him open his inner eyes and discover a spiritual key to come out of the ignorant prison that he had created within himself.

Are we willing to open your inner eyes? Are you willing to look into your core weaknesses? Are you willing to come out of the comfort of your ignorant prison?

Barber Nyaya

A King once wanted to know whose son was the best looking in the Kingdom. He thought about it. He felt that his own ministers' feedback, would not be truthful. Those around him too, would do it to please him. He thought about this for a while and decided that his barber would be a good person, for him to find the most handsome son in his kingdom, truthfully.

He called him over for a haircut. The barber arrived. As the barber began work, the King said, "I have a question for you. I want your frank answer."

The barber replied, "I'll do my best your Majesty. Please go ahead with whatever you may want to ask."

The King decided to add a twist. "After a haircut, whose son, amongst the ones you work on, looks most handsome in the kingdom? Please be frank. To be fair, I'll give you a month's time. Return, with the answer after that."

The King summoned him at the end of the month. "Have you decided?"

"Yes your Majesty," said he.

"Well, who's it?" asked the King.

"Your Majesty, it's none other than my son. He looks the best of the lot, after a haircut."

Infatuation victimised the barber!

Can you see how the barber was a victim of his infatuation?

Quite often, people operate from their experiences and expectations. It's own foolishness that limits and imprisons them.

Leadership Tips

Refer to the diagram below. There are inspirational insights in the listed key values. These are designed to motivate you and continuously engage yourself to progress in spiritual leadership. They'll also help you reach your goals to profitable growth.

The leader in you can create many leaders - you'll be the catalyst!

The current world needs you the most.

Leadership Equation:

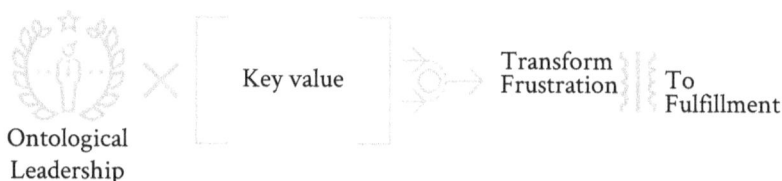

Ontological Leadership $\times$ Key value $\rightarrow$ Transform Frustration To Fulfillment

Some of the inspirational insights as key values are:-

Creativity	Ideation	Team Building	Accountability
Adaptability	Team Action	Mentoring	Tolerance
Receptivity	Attitude	Leadership	Openness
Flexibility	Perseverance	Contribution	Commitment
Responsibility	Let Go	Inclusiveness	Belief
Authenticity	Delegation	Empathy	Encouragement
Building Good Relationship	Mentoring	Mutual Respect	Welcoming Diversity

www.ingramcontent.com/pod-product-compliance
Lightning Source LLC
Chambersburg PA
CBHW031948080426
42735CB00007B/314